DISCIPLESHIP

IN HIS STEPS

AT A GLANCE

Serendipity House / P.O. Box 1012 / Littleton, CO 80160

TOLL FREE 1-800-525-9563 / www.serendipityhouse.com

© 1989, 1998 Serendipity House. All rights reserved.

SECOND EDITION

99 00 01 02 / **201 series • CHG** / 4 3 2 1

PROJECT ENGINEER:
Lyman Coleman

WRITING TEAM:
Richard Peace, Lyman Coleman, Matthew Lockhart, Andrew Sloan, Cathy Tardif

PRODUCTION TEAM:
Christopher Werner, Sharon Penington, Erika Tiepel

COVER PHOTO:
© 1998 R. Faris / Westlight

CORE VALUES

Community: The purpose of this curriculum is to build community within the body of believers around Jesus Christ.

Group Process: To build community, the curriculum must be designed to take a group through a step-by-step process of sharing your story with one another.

Interactive Bible Study: To share your "story," the approach to Scripture in the curriculum needs to be open-ended and right brain—to "level the playing field" and encourage everyone to share.

Developmental Stages: To provide a healthy program in the life cycle of a group, the curriculum needs to offer courses on three levels of commitment: (1) Beginner Stage—low-level entry, high structure, to level the playing field; (2) Growth Stage—deeper Bible study, flexible structure, to encourage group accountability; (3) Discipleship Stage—in-depth Bible study, open structure, to move the group into high gear.

Target Audiences: To build community throughout the culture of the church, the curriculum needs to be flexible, adaptable and transferable into the structure of the average church.

ACKNOWLEDGMENTS

To Zondervan Bible Publishers
for permission to use
the NIV text,
The Holy Bible, New International Bible Society.
© 1973, 1978, 1984 by International Bible Society.
Used by permission of Zondervan Bible Publishers.

Questions & Answers

STAGE

1. What stage in the life cycle of a small group is this course designed for?

Turn to the first page of the center section of this book. There you will see that this 201 course is designed for the second stage of a small group. In the Serendipity "Game Plan" for the multiplication of small groups, your group is in the Growth Stage.

GOALS

2. What are the goals of a 201 study course?

As shown on the second page of the center section (page M2), the focus in this second stage is equally balanced between Bible Study, Group Building, and Mission / Multiplication.

BIBLE STUDY

3. What is the approach to Bible Study in this course?

Take a look at page M3 of the center section. The objective in a 201 course is to discover what a book of the Bible, or a series of related Scripture passages, has to say to our lives today. We will study each passage seriously, but with a strong emphasis on practical application to daily living.

THREE-STAGE LIFE CYCLE OF A GROUP

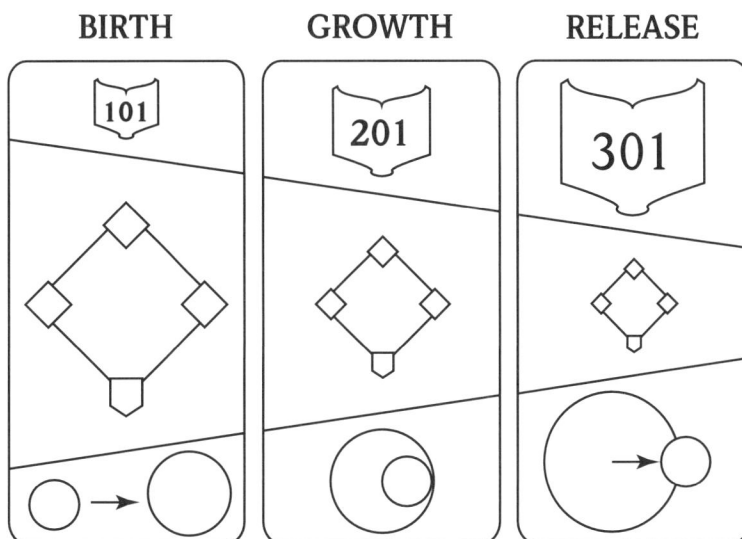

BIRTH	GROWTH	RELEASE
101	201	301

GROUP BUILDING

4. What is the meaning of the baseball diamond on pages M2 and M3 in relation to Group Building?

Every Serendipity course includes group building. First base is where we share our own stories; second base means affirming one another's stories; third base is sharing our personal needs; and home plate is deeply caring for each others' needs. In this 201 course we will continue "checking in" with each other and holding each other accountable to live the Christian life.

MISSION / MULTIPLICATION

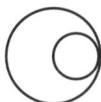

5. What is the mission of a 201 group?

The mission of this 201 Covenant group is to discover the future leaders for starting a new group. (See graph on the previous page.) During this course, you will be challenged to identify three people and let this team use the Bible Study time to practice their skills. The center section will give you more details.

THE EMPTY CHAIR

6. How do we fill "the empty chair"?

First, pull up an empty chair during the group's prayer time and ask God to bring a new person to the group to fill it. Second, have everyone make a prospect list of people they could invite and keep this list on their refrigerator until they have contacted all those on their list.

AGENDA

7. What is the agenda for our group meetings?

A three-part agenda is found at the beginning of each session. Following the agenda and the recommended amount of time will keep your group on track and will keep the three goals of Bible Study, Group Building, and Mission / Multiplication in balance.

THE FEARLESS FOURSOME!

If you have more than seven people at a meeting, Serendipity recommends you divide into groups of 4 for the Bible study. Count off around the group: "one, two, one, two, etc."—and have the "ones" move quickly to another room for the Bible Study. Ask one person to be the leader and follow the directions for the Bible Study time. After 30 minutes, the Group Leader will call "Time" and ask all groups to come together for the Caring Time.

ICE-BREAKERS | 8. *How do we decide what ice-breakers to use to begin the meetings?*

Page M7 of the center section contains an index of ice-breakers in four categories: (1) those for getting acquainted in the first session or when a new person comes to a meeting; (2) those for the middle sessions to help you report in to your group; (3) those for the latter sessions to affirm each other and assign roles in preparation for starting a new group in the future; and (4) those for evaluating and reflecting in the final session.

GROUP COVENANT | 9. *What is a group covenant?*

A group covenant is a "contract" that spells out your expectations and the ground rules for your group. It's very important that your group discuss these issues—preferably as part of the first session (see also page M32 in the center section).

GROUND RULES | 10. *What are the ground rules for the group?* (Check those you agree upon.)

❒ PRIORITY: While you are in the course, you give the group meetings priority.

❒ PARTICIPATION: Everyone participates and no one dominates.

❒ RESPECT: Everyone is given the right to their own opinion and all questions are encouraged and respected.

❒ CONFIDENTIALITY: Anything that is said in the meeting is never repeated outside the meeting.

❒ EMPTY CHAIR: The group stays open to new people at every meeting.

❒ SUPPORT: Permission is given to call upon each other in time of need—even in the middle of the night.

❒ ADVICE GIVING: Unsolicited advice is not allowed.

❒ MISSION: We agree to do everything in our power to start a new group as our mission (see center section).

Introduction to Life of Christ

Jesus in History

There has never been anyone else like Jesus Christ. That, of course, is obvious to the Christian. But consider the view of the non-believer for a moment. They may not believe in Jesus' extraordinary powers and his claim to be the Son of God. But they are still left with a question that has mystified historians and philosophers for 2,000 years: Who was this man called Jesus Christ?

No one doubts that Jesus has had a profound influence on the world—more so than any other person. His story is a major theme of Western history. In fact, the events of history are measured by whether they happened before (B.C.) or after (A.D.) his birth. Explorers like Christopher Columbus, settlers like the Pilgrims, and missionaries like the Moravians and Franciscans were driven by a desire to honor God and claim new territory for Christ's kingdom. Many of the greatest works of Western art and music were created to honor Christ. King Richard the Lion-Hearted and others declared holy wars in his name, and activists such as Ghandi and Martin Luther King led peaceful protests based on Christ's example of nonviolence. Even adherents of Hinduism and Islam honor him as a great teacher.

In spite of Jesus' great influence, however, there is still a sense of mystery surrounding him. Who was Jesus? What was he like? These simple questions prompt a dizzying array of responses.

Different views of Jesus are clearly seen in films made over the years. *The Greatest Story Ever Told* (1965) pictures Jesus as an otherworldly figure, somewhat oddly intersecting with the world as we know it. He speaks King James English while everyone else talks like an American! In *Jesus Christ: Superstar* (1973), Jesus is portrayed as a discontented hippie, prone to strong emotions and outbursts of passion. Misunderstood by everyone else, he is not quite sure of himself either. The film *Jesus* (1979) presents a wise, gentle Jesus who patiently deals with the confusion everyone else experiences, while being clearly in control of his destiny.

While only one of these films (*Jesus*) was produced by a religious group, it is clear that even within circles of committed Christians there is wide diversity in terms of the way people understand Jesus. The way Jesus has been portrayed throughout history in art and literature reflects this. No North American congregation today would feel very comfortable if the front of their church were decorated with a portrait of Jesus flanked by the president of the United States and his wife. Yet frescoes of Jesus standing with contemporary kings and queens were common in churches throughout Europe during the middle centuries. This not only reflected a different view of church and state than North Americans have today. It also reflected a view of an ethereal Jesus whose rule over the cosmos was accompanied by all the trappings of earthly, materialistic power.

Church mosaics from even earlier periods picture Jesus as a Roman soldier, his cross wielded in his right arm like a sword. He is a conqueror, the leader of the church in its domination of the world with the Gospel. In sharp contrast, the Russian author Dostoevsky, in his novel *The Brothers Karamazov,* tells a tale of Jesus as a prisoner being tried and tortured by the church itself!

Many white Protestant Christians have traditionally identified Jesus with the fair-skinned, blue-eyed, hair-freshly-shampooed figure portrayed by Warner Sallman's famous "Head of Christ." This picture, found in prominent places in many churches, shows a calm, quiet, handsome man who (if he got a haircut and put on a suit) could easily fit in any Presbyterian or Lutheran church in America. However, many African-American Christians have a hard time believing that such a Jesus could relate at all to them. Likewise, white North American Christians are taken aback at portrayals of Jesus as black or Chinese.

Charles Sheldon's book *In His Steps*, a best-selling novel written at the end of the nineteenth century, imagines Jesus as a teacher of common sense and decency. To practice his way of life was certain to lead to the social respect, economic security, and good government that Americans so valued. This Jesus, however, has little in common with the Jesus of the poor communities in Latin America. There he is seen as one who sides with the poor in speaking out against those same social, economic, and governmental forces of North America which survive, in part, by institutionalized oppression of the underdeveloped countries. The contrast is similar to the way the Jesus of the white slaveholders (in the southern states in the early 1800s) was different from the one worshiped by their slaves.

Perhaps by now the point has been established: coming to understand who Jesus is can be a difficult task! Everyone has some image of Jesus, through which they try to understand him. The questions, "Jesus Christ, Jesus Christ. Who are you? What have you sacrificed?"— which begin the theme song from the musical *Jesus Christ: Superstar*—continually need to be asked. Otherwise, we end up with a Jesus who is more a product of our culture than of Scripture.

Jesus in the Gospels

Jesus Christ: Superstar does not attempt to answer the critical questions which it raises, but the Gospels do. In fact, the Gospel of Mark— thought by most scholars to be the first Gospel—could be divided between these two questions: Mark 1–8 is built around the question, "Who is Jesus?" Chapters 9–16 look at the question, "Why did he come?"

The fact that the Gospel of Mark is framed to give insight to those two questions reveals something important about the Gospels. Although the Gospels are commonly thought of as biographies of Jesus, that is really not the case. A closer examination of the four Gospels reveals that the authors were not simply reporters, jotting down the day-to-day activities of Jesus. For instance, only Matthew and Luke have a birth narrative, and only Luke mentions anything at all about Jesus' childhood. John places the story of the raising of Lazarus as the climax of Jesus' identity and mission, yet none of the other Gospels even mention it. Some of the stories and teachings that the Gospels have in common are used to illustrate entirely different points. Close to a third of the material in each of the Gospels deals with the final week of Jesus' life.

This observation does not mean that the Gospels contradict one another or contain errors. What it does mean, however, is that the long-standing assumption that the Gospel authors were writing histories of Jesus is mistaken. It is far more useful to see the authors as theologians using narratives (or stories) as their means of teaching. As such, they were free to take the stories and sayings of Jesus (which were probably already well-known in the early church) and shape them in various ways to present Jesus in the way they felt their churches needed to see him. We simply do not have an untouched history of the life of Jesus. But what we do have are four Spirit-inspired character sketches of his life, teachings and significance.

Perhaps a modern-day analogy will help clarify the intent of the authors of the Gospels. When the Democrats and Republicans meet at their national conventions to present their candidate for president, there will inevitably be a multi-media show about the candidate. In 1996, scenes from the life of Bill Clinton and Bob Dole were flashed before our eyes. Their childhood, their accomplishments, and the people with whom they associate were all reflected in some way. The scenes were all true. The producers undoubtedly used real pictures of real events in these men's lives. Yet there was no attempt to present these pictures in chronological order because the productions were not meant to be historical biographies. The pictures were organized around themes, not time. Their purpose was to communicate something of the character of candidate Dole and candidate Clinton so that you and I would vote for him. Had another producer arranged the show, he or she might have used the same images in a totally different pro-

A slide presentation to present character, not history

7

gression in order to convey a different aspect of the candidate's personality. It would be foolish to say such presentations are false because scenes did not occur in chronological order. The producers never intended the show to be understood that way.

In the same way, the Gospel writers use scenes from the life of Jesus in order to present a picture of Jesus that will move their readers to respond in faith and obedience. Each Gospel is read as a separate work, each with its own perspective about who Jesus is and why he came.

The author of the fourth Gospel concluded by writing, "Jesus did many other things as well. If every one of them were written down, I suppose that even the whole world would not have room for the books that would be written" (John 21:25). Though exaggerated, the point is clear: that there was a wealth of information about Jesus that the author did *not* include! As a result, the stories we have about Jesus are not incidental. Each story is chosen and told in relation to the other stories in that Gospel to convey something either about the identity of Jesus or about the meaning of discipleship. Like the parables Jesus told or the miracles he performed, the incidents in the life of Jesus have a meaning beyond the story. The authors use these stories to provide theological insight regarding Jesus. In basic terms, the interests of each of the authors are as follows:

1. Matthew's interest is in showing that Jesus is the long-awaited Messiah. Notable in his narrative is the repeated phrase "this was to fulfill what was written …" by which he relates events in Jesus' life to Jewish prophecy (1:22; 2:5,17,23; 3:3; 4:14–16; 5:17–18; 8:17; 11:4–6; 12:17–21; 13:35; 21:4–5; 26:31). In addition, Matthew has five major blocks of teaching which form a manual about the kingdom of God (5:1–7:27: The Character of the Disciple; 10:1–42: The Preaching of the Kingdom; 13:1–52: Parables of the Kingdom; 18:1–35: Relationships in the Kingdom; 23:1–25:46: The Judgment of the Kingdom).

Matthew wants to help his fellow Jews understand Jesus as God's Messiah of the new kingdom, whom they should follow in discipleship.

2. Mark, the shortest Gospel, highlights the actions of Jesus as a means of demonstrating his identity. Mark's terse, fast-moving style compels the reader to see Jesus as a person of enormous authority. The realization of that keeps people amazed and asking the question, "Who is he?" (1:27; 2:7,12; 4:41; 5:20,42; 6:51; 7:37; 8:29). Mark wants his readers to see Jesus as the incarnate Lord, the "Son of God," who came to redeem people from sin.

3. Luke's concern is to stress that the coming of Jesus means good news for all peoples, especially those who are considered insignificant by their culture. Shepherds, children, women, and "sinners" of all types figure prominently. Luke alone tells the story of the sinful woman who anointed Jesus' feet with her tears (7:36–50) and includes the Parable of the Prodigal Son (15:11–32), both of which typify his interest in God's love for the "outsider."

4. John's Gospel is very different from the other three. The chronology is vastly different (as is his style). Jesus engages in long dialogues and monologues not found in the other Gospels. Seven miracles, most of which are not found in the other Gospels, form the framework upon which the author builds his Gospel. The death of Jesus is never far from view, even in the first chapter, in which Jesus is identified as "the Lamb of God, who takes away the sin of the world" (1:29). John wants his readers to see Jesus as God in the flesh (1:14; 8:58; 20:28); he has come to give his life so that all who entrust themselves to him might have life.

The fact that each Gospel has a different emphasis is an advantage for us. Our understanding of Jesus is broader than it could ever be if we had only one source. But sometimes we can become so preoccupied with the differences in the Gospels that we lose sight of the meaning. For instance, many writers have worked out a way to explain the seeming differences in the order of events in the life of Christ. But it is very important that we do not stop there. We need to interpret the stories in a given Gospel in light of the overall emphasis of that particular Gospel. Let each author tell his own story.

The Purpose of These Studies

Given this background, the studies in this book should not be approached as a "harmony" of the Gospels. While the material has been arranged in a logical order (beginning with Luke's birth story and ending with Matthew's account of the Resurrection), the point is not to try to present a *history* of Jesus. Instead, these studies are more like snapshots in a photograph album. Each snapshot tells an important story about Jesus. The notes accompanying each study provide some of the context to aid the reader's understanding of the story in relationship to the overall thrust of the particular Gospel in which it is found.

Reading the Gospels is not like reading other biographies. The study of these 13 selections from the Gospels will give the reader a sense of some of the important events in the life of Jesus. The main purpose of these passages is to lead readers into a greater understanding of the meaning of Jesus' life and its implications for their own. What may start as an interest in a famous person of history becomes an exercise in self-evaluation and decision making.

We will personally have to wrestle with the question, "Who is Jesus?" We will especially have to confront the ways in which our views of Jesus are more colored by our particular culture than by the meaning of the stories we have about him.

We will also have to wrestle with our response to Jesus. Too often people look to the Gospels (and the Bible as a whole) only as a source of comfort and assurance. In reality, a great deal of the Bible is meant to provoke precisely the opposite reactions! The Gospels do not give us the option of holding a polite, distant admiration of Jesus as a wonderful religious teacher. Instead, they call for us to think and live differently. We have to change, and be ready to keep on changing as the implications of discipleship unfold before us and become clear. A continual, thoughtful reading of the Gospels will not reinforce any long-held image of Jesus. The picture is more like looking at an object through a kaleidoscope. We will find a dynamic, multifaceted character whose identity and teaching cannot be captured by any one description.

The story is told of a British commentator who wrote an insightful article about the meaning of James 2:1–4. In this passage, James warns the church not to show favor toward the rich. For instance, James specifically attacks the custom of reserving the best seats for the wealthy, while the poor are made to stand in the back or sit on the floor. The commentator, upon completing a detailed exposition of this passage, concluded with the assurance that this teaching did not apply to the then-common practice in English churches of having the affluent members of the church sit in the best seats, while poorer members were kept in the back! The commentator's cultural blinders led him to deny what certainly appears to be precisely the point of the text for the life of the church!

It's easy to fault the commentator, but will we do better? Will we listen to the message of the Gospels, even when that message threatens *our* traditional assumptions and practices? That question presses in on us in a variety of ways throughout these stories, throughout the Gospels, and throughout all of Scripture. Reading and reflecting upon the life of Jesus is a dangerous habit! It will continually force us to deal with the basic challenge of the Christian faith: In light of what you understand about Jesus, how will you follow him now?

9

1 The Birth of Jesus—Luke 2:1–20

THREE-PART AGENDA

ICE-BREAKER
15 Minutes

BIBLE STUDY
30 Minutes

CARING TIME
15–45 Minutes

LEADER: Be sure to read pages 3–5 in the front of this book, and go over the ground rules on page 5 with the group in this first session. See page M7 in the center section for a good ice-breaker. Have your group look at pages M1–M5 in the center section and fill out the team roster on page M5.

TO BEGIN THE BIBLE STUDY TIME
(Choose 1 or 2)

1. What is your favorite Christmas carol?

2. If you are a parent, where was your oldest child born? Who was the first person you told?

3. What's the best news you've received lately? How did you get this news?

READ SCRIPTURE & DISCUSS
(If you don't have time for all the questions in this section, conclude the Bible Study [30 min.] by answering question #7.)

1. Where were you born? How long did you live there? How often do you go back? How long does it take to get there?

2. Pregnant before marriage. Poor. No place to stay. What chance would you have given this marriage?

2:19

3. How do you think Joseph and Mary felt about the timing of the census? Why was it important that Jesus be born in Bethlehem (see Micah 5:2)? p. 138

4. Of all the people the angels could have visited, why do you suppose God sent them to the shepherds?

The Birth of Jesus

2 *In those days Caesar Augustus issued a decree that a census should be taken of the entire Roman world. [2](This was the first census that took place while Quirinius was governor of Syria.) [3]And everyone went to his own town to register.*

[4]So Joseph also went up from the town of Nazareth in Galilee to Judea, to Bethlehem the town of David, because he belonged to the house and line of David. [5]He went there to register with Mary, who was pledged to be married to him and was expecting a child. [6]While they were there, the time came for the baby to be born, [7]and she gave birth to her firstborn, a son. She wrapped him in cloths and placed him in a manger, because there was no room for them in the inn.

[8]And there were shepherds living out in the fields nearby, keeping watch over their flocks at night. [9]An angel of the Lord appeared to them, and the glory of the Lord shone around them, and they were terrified. [10]But the angel said to them, "Do not be afraid. I bring you good news of great joy that will be for all the people. [11]Today in the town of David a Savior has been born to you; he is Christ the Lord. [12]This will be a sign to you: You will find a baby wrapped in cloths and lying in a manger."

[13]Suddenly a great company of the heavenly host appeared with the angel, praising God and saying,

[14]"Glory to God in the highest,
and on earth peace to men on whom his favor rests."

[15]When the angels had left them and gone into heaven, the shepherds said to one another, "Let's go to Bethlehem and see this thing that has happened, which the Lord has told us about."

[16]So they hurried off and found Mary and Joseph, and the baby, who was lying in the manger. [17]When they had seen him, they spread the word concerning what had been told them about this child, [18]and all who heard it were amazed at what the shepherds said to them. [19]But Mary treasured up all these things and pondered them in her heart. [20]The shepherds returned, glorifying and praising God for all the things they had heard and seen, which were just as they had been told.

5. What three titles are given to Jesus in verse 11? What is significant about them (see notes on v. 11)?

6. What do you treasure the most about Jesus?

7. What brought you to this study and what are you hoping to get out of it?

CARING TIME

1. Has your group agreed on its group covenant and ground rules (see page 5 in the front of this book)?

2. Have you filled out your team roster (see page M5 in the center section)? Like any winning team, every position needs to be covered.

3. Help to "spread the word" (v. 17) about the good news of Jesus. Who is someone you could invite to this group?

Share prayer requests and close in prayer. Be sure to pray for "the empty chair" (p. 4).

P.S. At the close, pass around your books and have everyone sign the Group Directory inside the front cover.

11

Notes—Luke 2:1–20

Summary. The story of Jesus begins with his birth. As Luke's account indicates, this was no ordinary birth. God was about to visit the planet. It is amazing that of all the ways God could have come—as the invincible King riding on a chariot of fire, as a Voice of Declaration out of the heavens, as a great Being of Light—he chooses to come as a helpless baby born of a woman. Thus the story begins with God's incarnation: the eternal, pre-existent Word of God becomes flesh and lives for a while among us (John 1:14).

This is the third of three visions of angels that are found in Luke's story of the birth of Christ (to Zechariah: 1:5–24; to Mary: 1:26–38; and to the shepherds: 2:8–20). The irony and grace of the Gospel is captured here as the angel declares the majesty and glory of Jesus and his mission to poor men and women of no status. The Lord of the universe is born in a stable to a peasant girl.

2:1 *Caesar Augustus.* Luke roots Christ's birth firmly in history. Augustus ruled the Roman Empire from 30 B.C. to 14 A.D. Originally known as Gaius Octavius (or Octavian), he was awarded the title Augustus (which means majestic or highly revered) by the Roman senate and became known thereafter as Caesar Augustus. Augustus was a wise ruler who encouraged the arts and built many fine projects. He also brought an unprecedented period of peace to the world.

> **The Lord of the universe is born in a stable to a peasant girl.**

census. From about 30 B.C. onward, the Caesars ordered people in the various Roman provinces to report every 14 years for a census for tax purposes. Resistance from the population and from local rulers sometimes meant census taking that took several years to complete.

2:3 *everyone went to his own town.* Generally people were taxed where they lived. If you had property elsewhere, however, you had to go there to register. So it seems that Joseph had some property in Bethlehem.

2:4 *Bethlehem.* Bethlehem was some 90 miles from Nazareth, a three or four day journey. Joseph was from the line of David and Bethlehem was the city of David, so this is where Joseph's family and clan would have lived (which is why he would have had property there).

2:5 *to register with Mary.* Normally only the head of the household needed to register. However, in some Roman provinces all women over 12 were required to pay a poll tax, and this may have been the reason Mary accompanied Joseph on this trip.

pledged to be married to him and was expecting a child. Their betrothal had not yet been consummated by intercourse (see Matt. 1:24–25). Luke 1:26–38 records the announcement by the angel to Mary that she would conceive a child through the agency of the Holy Spirit.

2:6–7 While in Bethlehem, the time for birth arrived. Thus the political decision of the Roman emperor led to the fulfillment of the prophecy in Micah 5:2: "But you, Bethlehem Ephrathah, though you are small among the clans of Judah, out of you will come for me one who will be ruler over Israel."

2:7 *firstborn.* The firstborn of every Jewish family was dedicated to God in a special way (Ex. 13:12; Luke 2:22–24).

manger. This was a feeding trough for animals.

the inn. This word can mean either a building used for the accommodation of travelers or a spare room in a private home. Whichever the case, there was no space available for the couple in normal lodgings. Instead, they stayed with the animals. A tradition dating back to the second century maintains this was in a cave over which today is the Church of the Nativity.

2:8 *shepherds.* Shepherds were economically, socially and religiously "low-class" people. Since the temple authorities kept flocks of sheep for sacrifices pastured near Bethlehem, it might be that the shepherds of these particular flocks were the ones visited by the angels. So it was to shepherds that the great announcement was made—not to kings nor to priests nor to the wealthy nor even to the religious—but it was to lower-class working men that the angel of the Lord appeared to announce the birth of the Savior.

2:9 *An angel of the Lord.* "The angel of the Lord … is represented as a heavenly being sent by God to deal with people as his personal agent and spokesman" (*The New Bible Dictionary*). In some Old Testament passages, the angel of the Lord is virtually identified as God himself (Gen. 16:7ff; Ex. 3:2; Judg. 6:11ff), indicating his divine authority and splendor. Popular thought often pictures angels as chubby, cute, naked children, but the Bible consistently represents them as supernatural creatures of enormous power and majesty. Throughout the Bible, angels serve as God's agents of instruction, judgment and deliverance.

the glory of the Lord. This is the overwhelmingly powerful light that accompanies the presence of God (Ps. 104:1–2; Ezek. 1).

they were terrified. In the Bible, whenever an angel appears, people are terrified. It is the fear of being in the presence of something supernatural, powerful, and totally foreign to one's experience (Luke 1:29–30; Ex. 3:2–6; Dan. 10:7).

2:10 *Do not be afraid.* The angel has not come to frighten them, but to announce God's good news to them.

I bring you good news of great joy. The form of the angel's message is similar to that used to announce the birth of Roman kings.

all the people. The Savior has come not just for Jews but for all people. This is an important theme in the Gospel of Luke. God's mercy includes the Gentiles; the Gospel is universal, not particular.

2:11 *a Savior … Christ the Lord.* The angel gives a full-orbed description of the roles which this child will play.

Savior. In the Old Testament, this term only applied to God (Isa. 43:3,11). God's deliverance of Israel (first from Egypt and then, centuries later, from Babylon) illustrates that the title is meant to honor God as the one who rescues his people from an otherwise unbeatable foe. This title was ascribed to Jesus as the one who saves his people from sin and death.

Christ. This is the Greek word for the Hebrew title, Messiah. Both terms mean "the Anointed One." In Jewish thought, this meant the prophesied king of Israel who would deliver Israel from bondage into an era of freedom, power, influence and prosperity.

Lord. This is a very common title used for God in the Old Testament. It implies both his absolute authority and his deity. In the New Testament, this is the most often used title for Jesus as well, emphasizing his deity and authority.

2:12 *a sign.* In the Old Testament, God sometimes granted signs that proved to people the reliability of his word.

2:13 *a great company of the heavenly host.* There is probably a lot of shame connected with this birth, because of rumors that the child is illegitimate. So instead of family to celebrate the birth, there is a great company of angels!

2:14 *Glory to God in the highest.* The angelic chorus sings of how Jesus' birth will bring honor to God and personal and relational harmony to people whom he has called.

peace to men on whom his favor rests. While older versions divide this phrase into two clauses (peace on earth / good will toward men), the NIV translation is to be preferred. There are not two statements of God's wishes for humanity, but a clear promise of peace to those who receive God's grace.

2:16–20 Luke records three responses to the news of Jesus' birth. The townspeople were amazed at the shepherds' strange story, while Mary meditated upon the significance of their report. The shepherds themselves praised God, since what they had found in Bethlehem was just what the angels had told them.

2:17 *they spread the word.* Luke is concerned throughout his Gospel (as well as in Acts) to show that the message of Christ is to be taken to all people. The shepherds become the first witnesses.

2:19 *Mary treasured up all these things and pondered them in her heart.* The words used to describe Mary's response indicate deep thought and reflection in an attempt to understand.

2:20 *returned, glorifying and praising God.* The shepherds' response is similar to the disciples' after the Resurrection and Ascension (Luke 24:52–53).

2 Baptism & Temptation—Matt. 3:13–4:11

THREE-PART AGENDA

ICE-BREAKER
15 Minutes

BIBLE STUDY
30 Minutes

CARING TIME
15–45 Minutes

 *LEADER: If there's a new person in your group in this session, start with an ice-breaker (see page M7 in the center section). Then begin the session with a word of prayer. If you have more than seven in your group, see the box about the "Fearless Foursome" on page 4. Count off around the group: "one, two, one, two, etc."—and have the "ones" move quickly to another room for the Bible Study.*

TO BEGIN THE BIBLE STUDY TIME
(Choose 1 or 2)

1. When did you learn how to swim?

✓ 2. What's the longest you've gone without food? How does hunger affect you?

3. If you are a parent, what about your child(ren) pleases you the most?

READ SCRIPTURE & DISCUSS
(If you don't have time for all the questions in this section, conclude the Bible Study [30 min.] by answering question #7.)

Before Jesus began his public ministry he was rather dramatically baptized and tempted.

1. What food is most tempting for you: Ice cream? Chocolate? Fast food? Pickles? Other?

2. When it comes to baptism, what does your church practice? What does baptism signify?

The Baptism of Jesus

¹³Then Jesus came from Galilee to the Jordan to be baptized by John. ¹⁴But John tried to deter him, saying, "I need to be baptized by you, and do you come to me?"

¹⁵Jesus replied, "Let it be so now; it is proper for us to do this to fulfill all righteousness." Then John consented.

¹⁶As soon as Jesus was baptized, he went up out of the water. At that moment heaven was opened, and he saw the Spirit of God descending like a dove and lighting on him. ¹⁷And a voice from heaven said, "This is my Son, whom I love; with him I am well pleased."

The Temptation of Jesus

4 *Then Jesus was led by the Spirit into the desert to be tempted by the devil. ²After fasting forty days and forty nights, he was hungry. ³The tempter came to him and said, "If you are the Son of God, tell these stones to become bread."*

⁴Jesus answered, "It is written: 'Man does not live on bread alone, but on every word that comes from the mouth of God.'ᵃ"

⁵Then the devil took him to the holy city and had him stand on the highest point of the temple. ⁶"If you are the Son of God," he said, "throw yourself down. For it is written:

" 'He will command his angels concerning you,
*   and they will lift you up in their hands,*
so that you will not strike your foot against a stone.'ᵇ "

⁷Jesus answered him, "It is also written: 'Do not put the Lord your God to the test.'ᶜ"

⁸Again, the devil took him to a very high mountain and showed him all the kingdoms of the world and their splendor. ⁹"All this I will give you," he said, "if you will bow down and worship me."

¹⁰Jesus said to him, "Away from me, Satan! For it is written: 'Worship the Lord your God, and serve him only.'ᵈ"

¹¹Then the devil left him, and angels came and attended him.

ᵃ4 Deut. 8:3   ᵇ6 Psalm 91:11,12   ᶜ7 Deut. 6:16   ᵈ10 Deut. 6:13

3. Why did Jesus want to be baptized? What do you think it meant to him to hear his Father say, "This is my Son, whom I love; with him I am well pleased" (v. 17)?

4. Under what kind of circumstances was Jesus tempted?

5. In what three ways did the devil tempt Jesus?

6. How did Jesus overcome the temptations of the devil?

7. In what area are you most likely to be tempted? What have you found helpful in overcoming temptation?

CARING TIME
(Choose 1 or 2 of these questions before taking prayer requests and closing in prayer. Be sure to pray for the empty chair.)

1. How comfortable do you feel sharing your struggles with this group?

2. Who is someone you could invite to this group?

3. How can the group help you in prayer this week?

P.S. Add new group members to the Group Directory inside the front cover.

15

Summary. Little is known of Jesus' childhood except for the story of his visit to the temple with his parents when Jesus was 12 years old (Luke 2:41–52). Beyond this we know nothing. However, certain nonbiblical texts sought to "fill in the gaps," as it were. They tell wondrous tales of Jesus as a little boy who made clay birds come alive and fly and turned his playmates into goats. These stories are clearly products of overworked imaginations and add nothing to our true knowledge of Jesus. In the Gospels, in fact, the story of Jesus jumps from his birth right to his ministry.

Matthew, Luke, and Mark all begin the public ministry of Jesus with his baptism and temptation. At his baptism, he is affirmed as God's beloved Son. Through the temptation he is portrayed as the true servant of God. He remains faithful to God's ways, unlike the Israelites who rebelled against God during their 40 years in the wilderness after the Exodus (Deut. 1:19–46).

3:13 *Then Jesus came.* Matthew 3:1–12 tells the story of John the Baptist, a prophet who called upon the Jews to repent and prepare themselves for the coming of the Lord. As a sign of repentance, he called upon people to be baptized. This was a radical demand. At that time, only Gentiles who were converting to Judaism had to be baptized (in order to wash away the "Gentile filth" with which they were associated). John's call pointed out that Jews needed cleansing and repentance every bit as much as any Gentile. In 3:11–12, John announces that his ministry is simply the prelude of the One to come, who will baptize people with the Holy Spirit and the fire of God's judgment. Immediately after this ringing witness, Jesus appears. He is the one to whom John has been pointing.

from Galilee to the Jordan. This was a journey of a few days. Galilee was a province to the north of where John was baptizing in the Jordan River, in the province of Judea.

baptized. Whether this was done by immersion, by pouring, or by sprinkling is uncertain. All were considered forms of ceremonial washings that could be generally called baptisms. By allowing himself to be baptized, Jesus both identifies with the sin of his people (prefiguring his death for sin a few years hence) and proclaims his radical allegiance to God (an allegiance that will be tested through his temptations).

3:14 *I need to be baptized by you.* How John recognized Jesus as the One to come is not mentioned.

3:15 *to fulfill all righteousness.* "In the context of Jesus' baptism, the word 'righteousness' refers to the righteousness of life which was demanded of those who accepted that baptism; by submitting to John's baptism, Jesus acknowledged this standard of righteousness as valid both for himself and for others, and affirms that he will realize it and establish it ('fulfill') as the will of God in the Kingdom" (Hill).

3:16 *like a dove.* Matthew uses the symbol of a dove to communicate the coming of the Holy Spirit. Just what happened can never be fully known. The dove was not a common symbol in first-century Israel. However, even if the nature of the event is uncertain, its meaning is clear: this is the promised anointing of the Messiah with the Holy Spirit (see Isa. 11:2; 42:1; 61:1).

3:17 *a voice.* Whether or not the voice is heard by the crowds is not clear. The form of the statement— "This is my Son"— seems to indicate that others may have heard it. These words are an unqualified affirmation of Jesus as he is about to launch his ministry. In the days ahead, it will be Jesus' task to make known to Israel who he is. The words of the voice combine several Old Testament passages that capture Jesus' role (God's royal Son—Ps. 2:7), his relationship to God (beloved—Gen. 22:2), and his mission (God's chosen Servant—Isa. 42:1).

I am well pleased. This phrase is borrowed from Isaiah 42:1, which speaks of God's delight in his servant. In Isaiah, the servant of the Lord is the one who suffers for the sake of the people. Popular thought of the time did not associate the role of the Messiah with that of the Suffering Servant.

4:1 *led by the Spirit.* The same Spirit who had come to Jesus in such affirming power, now sends him forth to this time of testing.

tempted. This word always means "test" in Matthew. This was a trial of strength in which Satan's intent was to get Jesus to renounce his identity as the anointed one of God.

the devil. Satan does not figure prominently *per se* in the Old Testament (although the New Testament identifies the serpent in the Garden of Eden as

Satan—Rev. 12:9; see also Job 1:6; Zech. 3:2). But in later Jewish thought (and in the New Testament) he is portrayed as an angel who has rebelled against God and is set against God's purposes and people.

4:2 *forty days.* Moses fasted for 40 days on Mount Sinai while receiving the commandments (Ex. 34:28), and Israel was in the wilderness 40 years (Deut. 8:2). Matthew pictures Jesus as the new Moses and the new Israel.

4:3 *The tempter came.* The Spirit led Jesus into the wilderness, but it is Satan who tests him. His challenges to Jesus come only after Jesus has entered a condition of physical weakness.

If you are the Son of God. "If" should be understood in the sense of "since." Satan begins by challenging the need for the Son of God to fast at all. Why not simply use his divine power to end his hunger? This was a temptation to verify the truth of what God had declared (3:17).

bread. Satan's suggestion is not evil in itself, but in the context of this test, it would be like Israel's complaining that God had not adequately met their needs in the desert (Ex. 16). Rather than trust God, the temptation is for Jesus to take matters into his own hands.

4:4 Jesus' response is drawn from Deuteronomy 8:3, which was originally a reflection on the meaning of the manna in the desert. True life is found not through food ("bread alone"), but through the words of God. Jesus will not heed Satan, but listen only to his Father. God, who brought manna to Israel, also led them to hunger so that they might learn dependence upon him alone. This was the reason for Jesus' time in the desert as well. Israel complained, but Jesus will trust God to provide when it is appropriate.

4:5 *the highest point of the temple.* Barclay says this would have been a point about 450 feet above the Kedron Valley. The temple was the focal point in Israel of God's love and power. The challenge is to prove this love and power by creating a peril from which only God can rescue him. This would be a display that would gain the attention of the people, who would then recognize that Jesus has the rightful claim to the title "Messiah."

4:6 *If you are the Son of God.* Once again the challenge is to demonstrate that Jesus is the Messiah.

For it is written. Satan now quotes Psalm 91:11–12 to prove his case. The difference in the way Jesus and Satan use Scripture is instructive. Jesus uses quotes that sum up central truths found throughout the Old Testament Scripture. Satan wrests this quote from its context to manipulate it to mean something very different. Psalm 91:11–12 is a promise that God will be with his people in the midst of difficult times. Satan misapplies this promise to try to get Jesus to do something that would be foolhardy in an attempt to force God to act.

4:7 Jesus recognizes the manipulative tactic of Satan and quickly responds with a quote from Deuteronomy 6:16. That verse refers to an incident from Exodus 17:1–7, in which the people essentially gave Moses an ultimatum to prove whether "the Lord is among us or not." Jesus refuses to question the presence and protection of God as Israel did.

4:8–9 The final temptation has to do with gaining the kingdoms of the world without suffering the coming agonies of the cross.

4:9 *All this I will give you.* Satan offers Jesus a painless, immediate way to power and fame. In fact, by his obedience to the Father, Jesus would become the King of kings possessing all authority and power (Ps. 2:8; Dan. 7:14).

if you will bow down and worship me. This would involve a definitive turning from God to Satan. While Israel turned to idols in the desert (Ex. 32), Jesus refuses to turn from God.

4:10 Jesus quotes Deuteronomy 6:13 to affirm his allegiance to God and to reject Satan's offer. Such loyalty precluded any consideration of Satan's means to gain that power. Satan had appealed to Jesus' legitimate needs (v. 3), his insecurities (vv. 6–7), and his ambitions (v. 8), but had failed to overcome Jesus' loyalty to God. In the face of that resolve, Satan was powerless to dissuade Jesus.

4:11 *angels came and attended him.* One function of the angels is to bring comfort and aid to God's people (Heb. 1:14). Thus prepared by his baptism and his temptation, Jesus begins his ministry (4:12–17).

3 Jesus' Early Ministry—Luke 4:14–30

THREE-PART AGENDA

ICE-BREAKER
15 Minutes

BIBLE STUDY
30 Minutes

CARING TIME
15–45 Minutes

> **LEADER:** Remember to choose an appropriate ice-breaker if you have a new person at the meeting (see page M7 in the center section), and then begin with a prayer. If you have more than seven in your group, divide into groups of four for the Bible Study (see the box about the "Fearless Foursome" on page 4).

TO BEGIN THE BIBLE STUDY TIME
(Choose 1 or 2)

1. As a child, what church did you go to? What did you like best about it?

2. What is your favorite Scripture passage?

3. When was a time you were fired or let go?

READ SCRIPTURE & DISCUSS
(If you don't have time for all the questions in this section, conclude the Bible Study [30 min.] by answering question #7.)

Jesus had been led by the Holy Spirit to be tempted in the desert. Having affirmed his loyalty and faithfulness to God, he emerges from the wilderness empowered by God's Spirit.

1. Where is your hometown—the place you grew up? Where was the hangout?

2. When have you felt either under- or over-estimated because of where you were from or who you were related to?

3. What was different about Jesus that caused the crowd to ask in verse 22, "Isn't this Joseph's son?" *his illegitimate son ...*

Jesus Rejected at Nazareth

14Jesus returned to Galilee in the power of the Spirit, and news about him spread through the whole countryside. 15He taught in their synagogues, and everyone praised him.

16He went to Nazareth, where he had been brought up, and on the Sabbath day he went into the synagogue, as was his custom. And he stood up to read. 17The scroll of the prophet Isaiah was handed to him. Unrolling it, he found the place where it is written:

*18"The Spirit of the Lord is on me,
   because he has anointed me
      to preach good news to the poor.
   He has sent me to proclaim freedom for the prisoners
      and recovery of sight for the blind,
   to release the oppressed,
19   to proclaim the year of the Lord's favor."*

20Then he rolled up the scroll, gave it back to the attendant and sat down. The eyes of everyone in the synagogue were fastened on him, 21and he began by saying to them, "Today this scripture is fulfilled in your hearing."

22All spoke well of him and were amazed at the gracious words that came from his lips. "Isn't this Joseph's son?" they asked.

23Jesus said to them, "Surely you will quote this proverb to me: 'Physician, heal yourself! Do here in your hometown what we have heard that you did in Capernaum.'"

24"I tell you the truth," he continued, "no prophet is accepted in his hometown. 25I assure you that there were many widows in Israel in Elijah's time, when the sky was shut for three and a half years and there was a severe famine throughout the land. 26Yet Elijah was not sent to any of them, but to a widow in Zarephath in the region of Sidon. 27And there were many in Israel with leprosy in the time of Elisha the prophet, yet not one of them was cleansed—only Naaman the Syrian."

28All the people in the synagogue were furious when they heard this. 29They got up, drove him out of the town, and took him to the brow of the hill on which the town was built, in order to throw him down the cliff. 30But he walked right through the crowd and went on his way.

4. What is Jesus' five-fold mission according to verses 18 and 19?

5. What was it Jesus said that turned the people's amazement (v. 23) into anger (v. 28)?

6. When was a time you felt rejected? How did you deal with it? How did Jesus deal with it?

7. Where do you find it hardest to be accepted? In what way do you need to "walk right through the crowd" (v. 28) and continue on God's way?

CARING TIME

(Choose 1 or 2 of these questions before taking prayer requests and closing in prayer. Be sure to pray for the empty chair.)

1. Does your group have a person for every position on the team roster (see page M5 in the center section)?

2. If you were to describe your last week in terms of weather, what was it like: Sunny? Cold? Rainy? Stormy? Other? What is the forecast for the coming week?

3. How can the group pray for you?

19

Summary. Having affirmed his loyalty and faithfulness to God in a way that Israel had not been able to do, Jesus emerges from the wilderness empowered by God's Spirit. By contrast, Israel's rebellion in her forty-day wilderness experience resulted in 40 years of wandering as a judgment from God.

As this passage shows, the response to Jesus' ministry was mixed. On the one hand, his ministry was highly popular with the crowds, as might be expected in a day in which there was little reliable medical care (and Jesus effectively healed a variety of diseases); in which little could be done about demon possession (and Jesus effectively cast out all manner of demons); and in which the rabbinic teaching was pedantic and boring (while Jesus was praised as a powerful teacher). On the other hand, he was opposed by the people in his own hometown (who scorned him as one who pretended—in their view—to be someone he could not possibly be) and the religious leaders (who feared Jesus because he did not follow their ways—see Session 5).

4:14 Galilee. From 4:14–9:50, Luke records Jesus' ministry in Galilee, a province about 50 miles long and 25 miles wide in the north of Palestine.

in the power of the Spirit. Just as the Spirit led Jesus into his time of testing (Matt. 4:1; Luke 4:1), so the Spirit now empowers Jesus' ministry. Luke especially emphasizes the role of Jesus as the bearer of God's Spirit in fullness.

news about him spread. Jesus' initial ministry of healing, exorcism and teaching (Mark 1:21–39) met with enormous popular support in Galilee.

4:15 synagogues. While the temple in Jerusalem was the religious center for all Jews, the community synagogue was the focal point of weekly worship and teaching. Jesus' initial ministry was as a well-received itinerant preacher teaching in synagogues throughout Galilee. It is in the light of stories of his healings and teachings that he comes to his hometown of Nazareth.

4:16–30 Matthew and Mark record a similar visit to Nazareth that occurred later on in Jesus' ministry in Galilee (Mark 6:1ff; Matt. 13:54ff). That, as well as internal clues such as the reference to an earlier ministry in the area (vv. 14–15,23), indicates that Luke does not intend for this scene to be understood as the first appearance of Jesus in Galilee,

but instead uses it to introduce crucial themes of Jesus' ministry which will be developed throughout the Gospel. Three such themes stand out: (1) The nature of Jesus' mission in proclaiming that he is the agent through which God's deliverance of his people will be accomplished (vv. 18–21); (2) The rejection Jesus will receive from many (vv. 28–29); and (3) The fact that the message of the kingdom of God is not restricted to Israel, but is for all kinds of people (vv. 24–27).

4:16 Nazareth. Nazareth, a town of about 20,000 people, was located in a hollow surrounded by hills.

the Sabbath. Each Sabbath, Jews would gather at the synagogue for a service of worship and instruction from the Scripture. There was a standard order governing which passages of the Law would be read, and the same may have been true about the reading from the Prophets as well. The synagogue had no formal clergy, so various men approved by the elders of the synagogue read and taught from the Scripture. Given Jesus' emerging reputation, it is not surprising that he was asked to read and teach.

4:18 The passage Jesus read was from Isaiah 61:1–2 (with the addition of a phrase from 58:6). Using the metaphors of people in prison, blindness and slavery, the prophet speaks of his God-given mission to proclaim freedom and pardon to people who are oppressed and burdened.

The Spirit of the Lord is on me. The ministry of a prophet of God is one empowered by God's Spirit.

to preach good news / to proclaim freedom / recovery of sight. In the context of the Isaiah passage, this was the news that God was going to deliver the Jews from their captivity in Babylon. In later Judaism, it became the hope for Israel's ultimate restoration and freedom from all oppressors. The "recovery of sight" in Isaiah's sense probably meant the renewal of hope that was lost through the destruction and deportation of the Jews, or the sense that prisoners who had long been locked up would now be free to see the light of day.

release the oppressed. These words are not found in either the Hebrew or Greek versions of Isaiah 61, but may be borrowed from a phrase in

Isaiah 58:6 as a commentary on the meaning of the "recovery of sight."

4:19 *the year of the Lord's favor.* This specifically refers to the Jubilee Year of Leviticus 25. Every 50 years, the Jews were to release their slaves, cancel all debts, and return land to the families of its original owners. While there is no record that the Jews ever kept that law, it became a symbol of the deliverance and new order of justice that God intended to bring about when he would right the wrongs suffered by his people (see Luke 1:51–55).

4:21 *Today this scripture is fulfilled.* The phrase is reminiscent of Mark 1:15, with its announcement that the "kingdom of God is near." In both cases, Jesus asserts that the new era foretold by Isaiah has begun because he has come to bring it about. Isaiah's language regarding restored sight and release from slavery was figurative. Jesus' healings and exorcisms (which had made him so popular) were literal pointers to the truth that the new era of God's deliverance had begun and would come to pass through him. He is the one who truly does give sight. He is the one who actually has the power to set people free from tyranny. Jesus is clear about his claim: he is God's appointed Messiah (see also Matt. 11:4–6). "This original 'today' has become part of the era of fulfillment, the 'year of the Lord's favor' which has now come and remains present (2 Cor. 6:2). … The 'today' of Jesus is still addressed to all readers of the Gospel and assures them that the era of salvation is present" (Marshall).

4:22 *All spoke well of him.* The Greek word *martureo*, which is translated in the positive sense in this verse, can also be translated "to condemn" or "to speak against," depending on its context (compare Acts 13:22 with Matt. 23:31)! The violent response later in this story (v. 28) shows that the final reaction toward Jesus was decidedly negative. Whether or not there was an initial positive reaction, the congregation quickly becomes shocked at the way Jesus is applying this passage to himself.

amazed. Likewise, this word can express admiration (Luke 7:9) or opposition (John 7:15).

the gracious words. This phrase is used in Acts 14:3 and 20:32 as an idiom for the Gospel message.

Joseph's son. This may be a slur, alluding to rumors of Jesus' illegitimacy (see also Mark 6:3). In stark contrast to God's declaration in Luke 3:22 (also Matt. 3:17) that Jesus is God's Son, the hometown people could only see Jesus as Joseph's boy. Who did this carpenter's son think he was anyway?

4:23 *Physician, heal yourself.* This proverb has both Greek and Arabic parallels. The doubt and cynicism of his hometown is seen in that they would not believe the stories they had heard elsewhere unless they could see further evidence. It is probable that the signs which Jesus had already given were not respected.

Capernaum. According to Mark's Gospel, this is the village in which Jesus first began to teach and heal (Mark 1:21ff).

4:24 *no prophet is accepted in his hometown.* This proverb (Mark 6:4; John 4:44) also has Greek parallels. It simply observes that the hardest place for a famous person to gain respect is among the people he or she grew up with. Jesus introduces it with "I tell you the truth," a phrase he uses when he wants his listeners to pay particular attention to what he is saying (Luke 12:37; 18:17,29; 21:32; 23:43). The irony is that while they will honor Isaiah as a prophet, they refuse to see the fulfillment of his word in Jesus.

4:25–27 While neither Elijah nor Elisha were rejected by their own people, their ministry extended to others outside of Israel as well. These stories, found in 1 Kings 17:1–18:2 and 2 Kings 5:1–27, illustrate that God has never limited his grace only to Israel. They further emphasize the point that if Nazareth (and, by extension, the Jews as a whole) will not receive Jesus with faith, then there are plenty of others (including Gentiles) who will. This was incendiary language!

4:28–29 Jesus' strong words, which implied that Gentiles were more worthy of God's grace than the people from Jesus' hometown, provoked such a strong response that a mob desired to kill him.

4:30 *he walked right through the crowd.* This illustrates the proper fulfillment of Psalm 91:11–12, which Satan had twisted in his temptation of Jesus (Luke 4:10–11; see the notes on Matthew 4:6 in Session 2). How Jesus did so is unclear.

4 Calling the Disciples—John 1:35–51

THREE-PART AGENDA

ICE-BREAKER
15 Minutes

BIBLE STUDY
30 Minutes

CARING TIME
15–45 Minutes

> *LEADER: If there's a new person in this session, start with an ice-breaker from the center section (see page M7). Remember to stick closely to the three-part agenda and the time allowed for each segment. Is your group praying for the empty chair?*

TO BEGIN THE BIBLE STUDY TIME
(Choose 1 or 2)

1. What nicknames have you had?

2. What town in your area or state tends to get picked on?

3. In high school, what extracurricular activities were you involved in? Did you tend to be a leader or follower?

READ SCRIPTURE & DISCUSS
(If you don't have time for all the questions in this section, conclude the Bible Study [30 min.] by answering question #7.)

Jesus never intended to conduct his ministry alone. This passage records the calling of the first disciples.

1. Who has been influential in your life as a role model or teacher?

2. Jesus was on a mission from God that would change history. Why would he choose *these* guys?

3. What helped Nathanael overcome his initial skepticism about Jesus?

Jesus' First Disciples

³⁵*The next day John was there again with two of his disciples.* ³⁶*When he saw Jesus passing by, he said, "Look, the Lamb of God!"* ³⁷*When the two disciples heard him say this, they followed Jesus.* ³⁸*Turning around, Jesus saw them following and asked, "What do you want?"*

They said, "Rabbi" (which means Teacher), "where are you staying?"

³⁹*"Come," he replied, "and you will see."*

So they went and saw where he was staying, and spent that day with him. It was about the tenth hour.

⁴⁰*Andrew, Simon Peter's brother, was one of the two who heard what John had said and who had followed Jesus.* ⁴¹*The first thing Andrew did was to find his brother Simon and tell him, "We have found the Messiah" (that is, the Christ).* ⁴²*And he brought him to Jesus.*

Jesus looked at him and said, "You are Simon son of John. You will be called Cephas" (which, when translated, is Peter).

Jesus Calls Philip and Nathanael

⁴³*The next day Jesus decided to leave for Galilee. Finding Philip, he said to him, "Follow me."*

⁴⁴*Philip, like Andrew and Peter, was from the town of Bethsaida.* ⁴⁵*Philip found Nathanael and told him, "We have found the one Moses wrote about in the Law, and about whom the prophets also wrote—Jesus of Nazareth, the son of Joseph."*

⁴⁶*"Nazareth! Can anything good come from there?" Nathanael asked.*

"Come and see," said Philip.

⁴⁷*When Jesus saw Nathanael approaching, he said of him, "Here is a true Israelite, in whom there is nothing false."*

⁴⁸*"How do you know me?" Nathanael asked.*

Jesus answered, "I saw you while you were still under the fig tree before Philip called you."

⁴⁹*Then Nathanael declared, "Rabbi, you are the Son of God; you are the King of Israel."*

⁵⁰*Jesus said, "You believe because I told you I saw you under the fig tree. You shall see greater things than that."* ⁵¹*He then added, "I tell you the truth, you shall see heaven open, and the angels of God ascending and descending on the Son of Man."*

4. In this passage, how many different titles are attributed to Jesus? Which title means the most to you?

5. Who was the person in your life that first told you about Jesus? What was your initial reaction?

6. When did Jesus become more than just a name to you?

7. What is one way you can follow Jesus more closely in the coming week?

CARING TIME

(Choose 1 or 2 of these questions before taking prayer requests and closing in prayer. Be sure to pray for the empty chair.)

1. Who can you reach out to, like Andrew and Philip did, and invite to this group to learn about Jesus?

2. What area in your life would you like to ask this group to hold you accountable?

3. How can your fellow disciples pray for you?

Summary. Jesus did not conduct his ministry all alone. He called 12 men to be his close companions. Others also became his disciples—for example, the 72 that he sent out ahead of him to the towns and places he was planning to visit (Luke 10:1–12). Certain women became his disciples as well, which was amazing in a day when women were not taken seriously. In this passage, Jesus meets some of the men he will later call as his disciples (see Mark 1:16–20; 3:13–19).

At first glance, this passage seems to be full of rather insignificant conversations. But it is full of allusions to the meaning of discipleship and to the identity of Jesus. The identity of Jesus is progressively revealed through a series of titles. He is called the Lamb of God (vv. 29,36); the Son of God (v. 49); Rabbi (vv. 38,49); the Messiah (v. 41); the King of Israel (v. 49); and the Son of Man (v. 51). The other Gospels make it clear that Jesus' true identity was not recognized early in his ministry. This points out that the author's intention here is not so much to give a chronological account of Jesus' first days of ministry, but to declare clearly Jesus' identity to his readers right from the beginning. The rest of the Gospel provides evidence through Jesus' miracles and his teachings as to why these titles are appropriate.

1:35 *John was there again.* This refers to John the Baptist, who was baptizing "at Bethany on the other side of the Jordan" (John 1:28).

two of his disciples. A disciple was simply a person who adhered to the teachings of a particular rabbi or inspired teacher. John the Baptist had enormous popular appeal, and had gathered many disciples from as far away as Alexandria in Egypt to Ephesus in present-day Turkey (Acts 18:24–19:3).

1:36 *the Lamb of God.* Raymond Brown notes that the author may intend two possible allusions: (1) To the Passover ritual, in which a lamb was killed so that the wrath of God would "pass over" the home of the Israelites in Egypt (Ex. 12:1–23); or (2) To Isaiah's Suffering Servant "led like a lamb to the slaughter" (Isa. 53:7) as he "took up our infirmities" (Isa. 53:4).

1:38 *What do you want?* The motivation of those who would follow him is a concern for Jesus (John 2:24; 6:26). Discipleship requires a person to declare clearly his or her intentions.

Rabbi. Rabbis were teachers who gathered disciples around them. This is the recognition of Jesus' teaching authority.

where are you staying? This is the same word translated in verse 33 as "remain." The concern in this question is on Jesus' true dwelling place (his divine identity). In this Gospel, recognition of who Jesus is depends on knowing where he is from and where he is going (John 8:21; 9:30; 14:2–6).

1:39 *Come ... and you will see.* John's Gospel is fond of language that has double meanings. On the one hand, this appears to be a simple invitation to accompany Jesus to his residence. On the other hand, by this statement Jesus invites these followers to enter into the journey of discipleship with him. Only as they commit themselves to follow him will they perceive the nature of his true home and identity.

the tenth hour. Daytime began at about 6 a.m., so this was about 4 p.m.

1:41 *Andrew / Simon.* Although the implication is that all of this happens in Judea near the Jordan River (see v. 43), there is no record in the other Gospels that Jesus first met Simon Peter outside of Galilee. His presence in Judea in this Gospel suggests that Peter may have been a follower of John the Baptist as well (or at least someone who traveled to Judea in order to be baptized by John as a sign of his repentance). It is probable that the disciples' decision to follow Jesus actually was the result of several encounters that led them to the conclusion that he was one in whom they wished to invest their lives (see Mark 1:16–20).

We have found the Messiah. This is another title the author uses to identify Jesus. The Messiah was the one the people of Israel expected would be sent from God to deliver them from their oppression by Rome and restore Israel to its former greatness as a nation. He would be like the ancient King David, a powerful king who would rally his people together in a fight for freedom. Jesus poured a new meaning into this word. He taught that the deliverance he came to bring was a deliverance from sin that would usher in the kingdom of God.

that is, the Christ. This parenthetical expression is the author's commentary to his readers as he translates the Hebrew term "Messiah" into its Greek equivalent "Christ."

1:42 Cephas. The Aramaic name Cephas and the Greek name Peter both mean "rock." Although Peter sometimes seemed both inconsistent and uncertain during Jesus' time with him (John 18:15–17,25–27), Peter became the chief spokesman for the apostles after Jesus returned to heaven and the Holy Spirit came at Pentecost (Acts 2:14). The implication is that the decision to come to Jesus is one that will change a person from the inside out, producing a new character.

1:43 Galilee. So far the story has centered in Judea. Galilee, where Jesus spent his boyhood, was a province 60 miles north of Jerusalem. One of the reasons the Pharisees rejected Jesus' claim to messiahship was because they assumed he was born in Galilee. On the basis of Micah 5:2, they expected the Christ to be born in Bethlehem (see John 7:41,52).

1:44 Bethsaida. This was a village on the Sea of Galilee.

1:45 Nathanael. Like Andrew, Philip's response to discovering Jesus was to tell someone else. While Philip is found in the list of apostles mentioned in the other Gospels, Nathanael is not. It may be that he also bore the name Bartholomew, since in the other Gospels Philip and Bartholomew are mentioned together (i.e., Mark 3:18). It is also possible that he may not have been one of the apostles at all.

about whom the prophets also wrote. This refers to the common Old Testament expectation that God would send a leader who would save his people (i.e., Isa. 11:1–9; Mic. 5:2).

1:46 Nazareth! Nazareth was a small, insignificant village in Galilee. Undoubtedly, it seemed impossible to Nathanael that anyone important could come from there.

1:47 a true Israelite. Jesus' greeting implies an awareness of Nathanael's spiritual motivations reflected in that Nathanael, unlike Israel as a whole, came to Jesus. Israel was to be a people prepared to respond to God, but for the most part the nation failed to reflect that purpose.

in whom there is nothing false. This was not flattery, nor blindness to the fact that Nathanael had faults. Rather, it's a statement affirming Nathanael's sincerity and openness to God. He is an example of someone "pure in heart" (Matt. 5:8) in that, unlike so many others (see John 1:11), he truly seeks to know and follow God.

1:48 I saw you. This accents the supernatural knowledge of Jesus.

1:49 Son of God. This is a royal title used in the Old Testament to refer to Israel's kings who were called God's "Sons," in that they had the right and power, under God, to exercise authority over the people (see Ps. 2:1–8). The author applies this to Jesus, who, by virtue of his existence before creation and his identity with God (John 1:1–2), is God's Son in a unique sense. This title focuses on his authority and unique intimacy with the Father.

King of Israel. Given that "The Son of God" was a royal title, this is a complimentary way of making the same affirmation. Yet even during the times of the kings, God was always considered the real King of Israel (Ps. 95:3, Isa. 44:6). Jesus has come to lead Israel to the fulfillment of God's plans for the people.

1:50 greater things. This is probably an allusion to the miracles Jesus will perform as signs of his divinity, culminated by the grand miracle of his resurrection from the dead.

1:51 This recalls Jacob's dream (Gen. 28:10–12), with the significant difference that Jesus replaces the ladder as the means of communication between heaven and earth. The new Bethel (house of God) is found in Jesus himself. This anticipates the theme of John 2:19–21 (that Jesus is the new temple through whom worship is to be offered).

you. This is a plural term referring to all who believe, not just Nathanael.

the Son of Man. Of all the titles for Jesus in this chapter, this is the one Jesus uses of himself. Daniel 7:13ff provides for its background. The Son of Man is the One invested with divine authority to rule the earth, but it was not a commonly used term for the Messiah in Jesus' time. He may have used it precisely because it did not invoke the narrowly nationalistic stereotypes of the Messiah.

5 Jesus & Pharisees—Mark 2:13–22; 3:1–6

THREE-PART AGENDA

ICE-BREAKER
15 Minutes

BIBLE STUDY
30 Minutes

CARING TIME
15–45 Minutes

LEADER: If there's a new person in this session, start with an ice-breaker from the center section (see page M7). Remember to stick closely to the three-part agenda and the time allowed for each segment. Is your group praying for the empty chair?

TO BEGIN THE BIBLE STUDY TIME
(Choose 1 or 2)

1. What is your favorite thing to do on a Sunday?

2. What is your worst experience with the IRS?

3. Growing up, what was something you weren't allowed to do on Sunday?

READ SCRIPTURE & DISCUSS
(If you don't have time for all the questions in this section, conclude the Bible Study [30 min.] by answering question #7.)

The Pharisees were a small but powerful religious sect. Their prime concern was knowing and keeping the Old Testament Law in all its detail.

1. When you were growing up, what people were you told not to associate with?

2. Why did Jesus attend a dinner party with a bunch of tax collectors and "sinners"?

3. What point is Jesus making with the two stories in Mark 2:21–22 (see note)?

Matthew

¹³*Once again Jesus went out beside the lake. A large crowd came to him, and he began to teach them.* ¹⁴*As he walked along, he saw Levi son of Alphaeus sitting at the tax collector's booth. "Follow me," Jesus told him, and Levi got up and followed him.*

¹⁵*While Jesus was having dinner at Levi's house, many tax collectors and "sinners" were eating with him and his disciples, for there were many who followed him.* ¹⁶*When the teachers of the law who were Pharisees saw him eating with the "sinners" and tax collectors, they asked his disciples: "Why does he eat with tax collectors and 'sinners'?"*

¹⁷*On hearing this, Jesus said to them, "It is not the healthy who need a doctor, but the sick. I have not come to call the righteous, but sinners."*

¹⁸*Now John's disciples and the Pharisees were fasting. Some people came and asked Jesus, "How is it that John's disciples and the disciples of the Pharisees are fasting, but yours are not?"*

¹⁹*Jesus answered, "How can the guests of the bridegroom fast while he is with them? They cannot, so long as they have him with them.* ²⁰*But the time will come when the bridegroom will be taken from them, and on that day they will fast.*

²¹*"No one sews a patch of unshrunk cloth on an old garment. If he does, the new piece will pull away from the old, making the tear worse.* ²²*And no one pours new wine into old wineskins. If he does, the wine will burst the skins, and both the wine and the wineskins will be ruined. No, he pours new wine into new wineskins." ...*

3 *Another time he went into the synagogue, and a man with a shriveled hand was there.* ²*Some of them were looking for a reason to accuse Jesus, so they watched him closely to see if he would heal him on the Sabbath.* ³*Jesus said to the man with the shriveled hand, "Stand up in front of everyone."*

⁴*Then Jesus asked them, "Which is lawful on the Sabbath: to do good or to do evil, to save life or to kill?" But they remained silent.*

⁵*He looked around at them in anger and, deeply distressed at their stubborn hearts, said to the man, "Stretch out your hand." He stretched it out, and his hand was completely restored.* ⁶*Then the Pharisees went out and began to plot with the Herodians how they might kill Jesus.*

4. Why did Jesus heal the man in the synagogue when he did? *read 23-27*

5. Why did the Pharisees want to kill Jesus? Who would you say are the modern-day Pharisees?

6. What can this group do to ensure that it and the church are concerned with "the sick" and not just following religious rules and regulations?

7. How can you and this group reach out to "sinners" and people considered unacceptable?

CARING TIME

(Choose 1 or 2 of these questions before taking prayer requests and closing in prayer. Be sure to pray for the empty chair.)

1. What do you look forward to the most about these meetings?

2. How is your relationship with Jesus right now: Close? Distant? Improving? Strained? Other?

3. How can the group pray for you this week?

Getting to know their hearts.

27

Summary. In Session 3, we encountered the beginning of opposition to the ministry of Jesus. The reaction against him in Nazareth was unusual, however, since most of the people were quite enthusiastic about Jesus. His real opposition came from the religious leaders. In the three stories that follow, we see them probe Jesus ("Is he one of us?"), question Jesus ("Does he abide by our unwritten laws?"), and then come to the awful conclusion that not only is Jesus dangerous, he needs to be killed (Mark 3:6).

In this session, we will study three stories that Mark tells in order to show the nature of (and reason for) the opposition by the religious leaders. They are set in contrast to a previous series of stories (Mark 1:16–45) that show how popular Jesus was with the common people. News about Jesus has spread everywhere (Mark 1:28,45). It is not surprising, therefore, that the religious leaders want to know who he is and what he stands for.

2:13–17 In this story, the religious leaders question Jesus about his adherence to ritual law (in this case, eating with those who are considered "unclean"). In this story, Jesus also chooses another disciple.

2:14 *Levi.* Elsewhere he is identified as Matthew (Matt. 9:9), the disciple who eventually wrote one of the Gospels. By all counts Matthew was a poor candidate for a disciple. In his role as tax collector, he was hated by both the religious establishment and the common people.

tax collector's booth. Considered as vile as robbers or murderers, tax collectors in Galilee were seen by their fellow Jews as traitors, because they collaborated with the Roman power in order to become wealthy. Since only the tax collector knew the tax rate required by Rome, he was free to charge whatever the market would bear. Once he paid what he owed Rome, the rest was his to keep.

Follow me. In Matthew, Mark, and Luke, this is the key phrase regarding discipleship. Only those who leave their past behind to follow Jesus in faith and obedience are his disciples. While we are not told what else transpired that moved Matthew to respond this way, the crucial point is that he did choose to turn away from his past loyalties to pursue the way of Jesus.

2:15 *having dinner.* To share a meal with another was a significant event, implying acceptance of that person. In this way, Jesus extends his forgiveness to those who were seen as standing outside orthodox religious life.

"sinners." This was a slang phrase for those who failed to observe religious practices. These were generally the common people who had to work for a living and thus did not have enough time to keep all the ritual law (e.g., they did not wash their hands in a special, complicated way before a meal). If an upper-class daughter married a common man she was thought to have wed the equivalent of a wild beast (and was thus disowned by her family). Since these particular "sinners" associated with tax collectors, it is likely that they, too, were cut off from "proper" society.

2:16 *Pharisees.* This was a small but powerful religious sect (about 6,000 members at the time of Herod). Its prime concern was knowing and keeping the Law in all its detail. In their sincere effort to do this, Pharisees often became rigid, censorious, and deaf to the voice of God.

Why does he eat with tax collectors and "sinners"? They could not understand how a truly religious person could eat with people whose moral life was disreputable, and who ate food that was prepared and served in ways that violated the practices regarding ritual cleanliness.

2:17 Jesus responds by way of a metaphor laced with irony. At first glance, the Pharisees would perhaps have considered this a reasonable explanation of his behavior: he came to heal those who were sick—which to them meant the "sinners" with whom he ate. In later reflection they might come to wonder if perhaps Jesus considered them the sick ones! Jesus' response puts a twist on a proverb that was used to describe the mission of a holy person. The Pharisees would see their role in a similar way. They were to teach the people the ways of God. They did so by separating themselves from common people in order to set an example of religious and ceremonial holiness that others might be moved to follow. Holiness to them was defined as conforming to ritual law and tradition. In contrast, Jesus defined holiness as a way of relating to God and others, and chose to befriend "sinners" in their present circumstances.

When Matthew tells this story, he adds one more verse containing a quotation from Hosea 6:6 which says, "For I desire mercy, not sacrifice." This sheds light on how Jesus will go about healing the "sick" to whom he has been sent. It is through mercy, not through requiring more observance of religious ritual. Jesus' ministry to the outcasts (an act of mercy) is more pleasing to God than the rigid observance of law on the part of the Pharisees (a type of sacrifice).

2:18–22 The next question has to do with ritual law—in this case, the issue of fasting.

2:18 John's disciples. These are followers of John the Baptist.

fasting. Although the Old Testament Law did not require it, the Pharisees did not eat from 6 a.m. to 6 p.m. on Mondays and Thursdays as an act of piety. Regular fasting was assumed to be part of any serious religious discipline. The implication of the question is that there is something deficient about Jesus' disciples, because they do not observe rituals of fasting.

2:19–20 Jesus uses a brief parable to make his point. It would be entirely inappropriate for wedding guests to mourn when the groom appears! For the really poor there were few events to break the monotony and tedium of their lives. Marriage was one such occasion. Rather than go on a honeymoon, a Jewish couple stayed with their friends for a week-long feast during which everyone was released from all religious obligations, including fasting. Jesus implies that fasting (a sign of mourning) is inappropriate because he is on the scene. This enigmatic parable is loaded with implications, since God, in the Old Testament, is often referred to as the bridegroom of Israel.

2:20 the bridegroom will be taken from them. This ominous note, which does not fit with anyone's common ideas about what happens at a wedding, foreshadows Jesus' death. It will be as if the groom is suddenly, violently abducted just prior to his wedding.

2:21–22 Jesus uses two more mini-parables to emphasize his point. A piece of unshrunk cloth sewn to an old garment will pull apart when washed. New wine as it ferments and expands will burst old, inflexible wineskins. Likewise, Jesus' new way is not compatible with the traditions and rituals of the Pharisees. His way differs from theirs not only in degree, but in kind.

3:1–6 In the final incident in these five confrontation stories (Mark 2:1–3:6), the religious leaders come to a conclusion about Jesus: he is dangerous and so must die.

3:2 they watched him closely. By this time the religious leaders no longer questioned Jesus. Now they simply watched to see if his actions showed a disregard for law.

if he would heal him on the Sabbath. The issue is not healing, but whether Jesus would heal on the Sabbath in defiance of the oral tradition of the rabbis (which allowed healing only if there was danger to life). Jesus could have waited until the next day to heal this long-paralyzed hand.

3:4 Jesus asked them. Jesus began this section with a question (Mark 2:8–9) and ends it with another. The religious leaders may have been investigating Jesus, but Jesus was also getting to know their hearts.

3:5 anger / deeply distressed. Once again, Mark identifies the emotions of Jesus (see Mark 1:41). Jesus felt strongly about the injustice of a system that sacrificed the genuine needs of people for the traditions of men—all in the name of piety.

stubborn hearts. Just as they have come to a conclusion about him (see Mark 3:6), he has come to understand them. Their problem is that their hearts (the center of their beings) have calcified. The Greek word translated "stubborn" is also used to describe a gallstone or a tooth. Later Jesus will indicate that the disciples have the same problem (Mark 6:52; 8:17)!

"Stretch out your hand." Just as he deliberately declared the paralytic's sins forgiven (knowing that this was blasphemy to the teachers of the Law), here he deliberately heals on the Sabbath (knowing that this too was anathema to his critics).

3:6 Herodians. A political group made up of influential Jewish sympathizers of King Herod. They were normally despised by the Pharisees, who considered them traitors (for working with Rome) and irreligious (i.e., unclean). However, the Pharisees have no power to kill Jesus. This must come from civil authority, and hence the collaboration.

THREE-PART AGENDA

ICE-BREAKER	BIBLE STUDY	CARING TIME
15 Minutes	30 Minutes	15–45 Minutes

> *LEADER: Check page M7 in the center section for a good ice-breaker, particularly if you have a new person at this meeting. Is your group working well together—with everyone "fielding their position" as shown on the team roster on page M5?*

TO BEGIN THE BIBLE STUDY TIME
(Choose 1 or 2)

1. How sick do you have to be before you will go to the doctor?

2. What is one of your favorite sounds (e.g., laughter, rain, a distant train whistle)?

3. What miracle have you witnessed?

READ SCRIPTURE & DISCUSS
(If you don't have time for all the questions in this section, conclude the Bible Study [30 min.] by answering question #7.)

In spite of opposition from the religious establishment as seen in the last session, Jesus continues to heal people.

1. What is the nearest you, or someone close to you, have come to death and survived?

2. What did the ruler, the sick woman and the blind men have in common? How did Jesus respond to that?

3. Why did Jesus warn the men who had been blind not to say anything (v. 30)?

A Dead Girl and a Sick Woman

18While he was saying this, a ruler came and knelt before him and said, "My daughter has just died. But come and put your hand on her, and she will live." 19Jesus got up and went with him, and so did his disciples.

20Just then a woman who had been subject to bleeding for twelve years came up behind him and touched the edge of his cloak. 21She said to herself, "If I only touch his cloak, I will be healed."

22Jesus turned and saw her. "Take heart, daughter," he said, "your faith has healed you." And the woman was healed from that moment.

23When Jesus entered the ruler's house and saw the flute players and the noisy crowd, 24he said, "Go away. The girl is not dead but asleep." But they laughed at him. 25After the crowd had been put outside, he went in and took the girl by the hand, and she got up. 26News of this spread through all that region.

Jesus Heals the Blind and Mute

27As Jesus went on from there, two blind men followed him, calling out, "Have mercy on us, Son of David!"

28When he had gone indoors, the blind men came to him, and he asked them, "Do you believe that I am able to do this?"

"Yes, Lord," they replied.

29Then he touched their eyes and said, "According to your faith will it be done to you"; 30and their sight was restored. Jesus warned them sternly, "See that no one knows about this." 31But they went out and spread the news about him all over that region.

32While they were going out, a man who was demon-possessed and could not talk was brought to Jesus. 33And when the demon was driven out, the man who had been mute spoke. The crowd was amazed and said, "Nothing like this has ever been seen in Israel."

34But the Pharisees said, "It is by the prince of demons that he drives out demons."

4. In the four miracles from this passage, what is it that Jesus restores? What does this tell you about Jesus?

5. When Jesus casts out a demon, what is the reaction of the crowd? The Pharisees? You?

6. In what area of your life is it most difficult for you to have faith?

7. Where could you use a miracle in your life right now?

CARING TIME

(Choose 1 or 2 of these questions before taking prayer requests and closing in prayer. Be sure to pray for the empty chair.)

1. Are all the players on the team roster fulfilling the assignments of their position? (Look at the roster again on page M5 of the center section.)

2. What is something you feel God may be calling you to do?

3. How can the group pray for Jesus' healing touch for you or someone you know?

Summary. Opposition or not, Jesus' ministry flourished. While the leaders railed at him for not being religiously orthodox, Jesus simply went about healing people. In the face of his powerful healings, the words of his critics could not prevail in the hearts and minds of the crowds.

The four miracles in this passage show Jesus restoring health, life, sight and speech. As with the other miracles in this section of Matthew's Gospel (8:1–9:38), these miracles are not simply meant to impress Matthew's readers with Jesus' power. They are meant to be pointers to Jesus' identity as the Servant of God who has come to establish the new order of God's kingdom (see Isa. 61:1–3). The very nature of his healings provides insights regarding what the kingdom of God will be like when it is fully revealed. It is a realm of restoration and life. In God's kingdom there is freedom from all types of forces that oppress and destroy. It is a realm inaugurated by Jesus the Messiah. The first three stories stress the importance of faith in Jesus as the means of entering into the goodness of God's realm. The final story reveals the crisis of decision which Jesus produces: while some are amazed and proclaim his praises, others slander and insult him as the devil himself.

9:18 *a ruler.* Mark and Luke indicate that this man was the ruler of the local synagogue. In first-century Israel, the temple in Jerusalem was the sole place for sacrifice and was attended by numerous priests and other officials. In contrast, synagogues were found in each city and town where people met weekly on the Sabbath for worship and instruction. Synagogues were run by a committee of lay people (the rulers) who were responsible for the care of the building and for arranging services.

knelt before him. In contrast to the skepticism and criticism of the religious authorities in the passages just prior to this story (see Session 5), this man comes with reverence and respect for Jesus. In light of the opposition Jesus has received from the official leaders of the people, it could not have been easy for this man, a leader in his community, to humble himself before Jesus in this way. However, his concern for his daughter outweighed his pride.

put your hand on her. The laying on of hands was a common practice used for ordination, for blessing, and for healing.

9:20–22 As Jesus travels to the man's home, he is met by a woman with a chronic illness.

9:20 *a woman who had been subject to bleeding.* This woman was probably hemorrhaging from the womb. In addition to the obvious physical weakness such a chronic problem would produce, this particular problem rendered her ritually impure or unclean (see Lev. 15:25–30). As a result, she was not allowed to take part in temple worship, was unable to have any sexual relations with her husband, and was not supposed to be present in a crowd where others might brush up against her and also become "unclean." The long-term effects of this stigma must have eroded her marriage, her self-concept, and her relationship with God.

9:21 *touch his cloak.* Somehow, this woman had heard of Jesus' power and took the chance that he might heal her. Perhaps out of fear of rejection because she was "unclean," she did not even dare approach Jesus openly like the ruler. She simply wanted to touch his cloak without drawing any attention to herself at all. In a quasi-magical way, the power of a person was thought to be transferred to his or her clothing. The ruler thought that his daughter could be healed by Jesus' touch (v. 14). This woman thought she could be healed by touching his clothing.

9:22 *Take heart, daughter.* Jesus not only had power to heal her body; his words are intended to heal her spirit as he affirms her as a true child of God.

your faith has healed you. It was her faith that impelled her to reach out to Jesus—the source of healing power. Jesus' words point out that there is no magic involved in his healing. It is a matter of God's response to her faith in reaching out to him. The word Jesus uses to tell her that she is healed comes from the same root as the words "salvation" and "Savior." Spiritual as well as physical healing is in view here.

9:23 *flute players and the noisy crowd.* These were in all likelihood professional mourners. Even the poorest person was required to hire at least two flutes and one wailing woman to mourn a death. They are a sign that everyone felt that the child was dead.

Leadership Training Supplement

YOU ARE
HERE

BIRTH	GROWTH	RELEASE
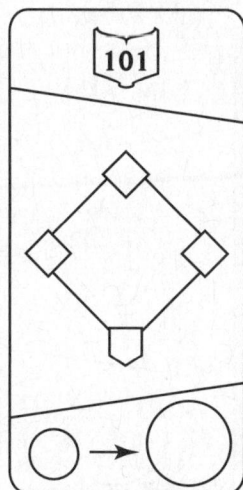	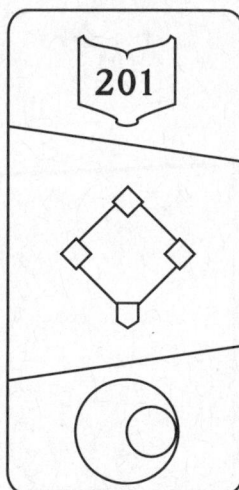	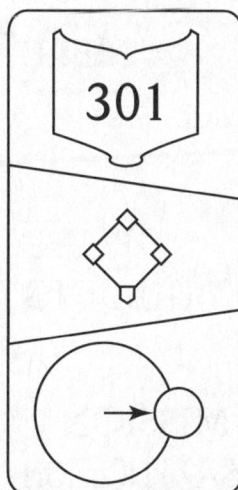

What is the game plan for your group in the 201 stage?

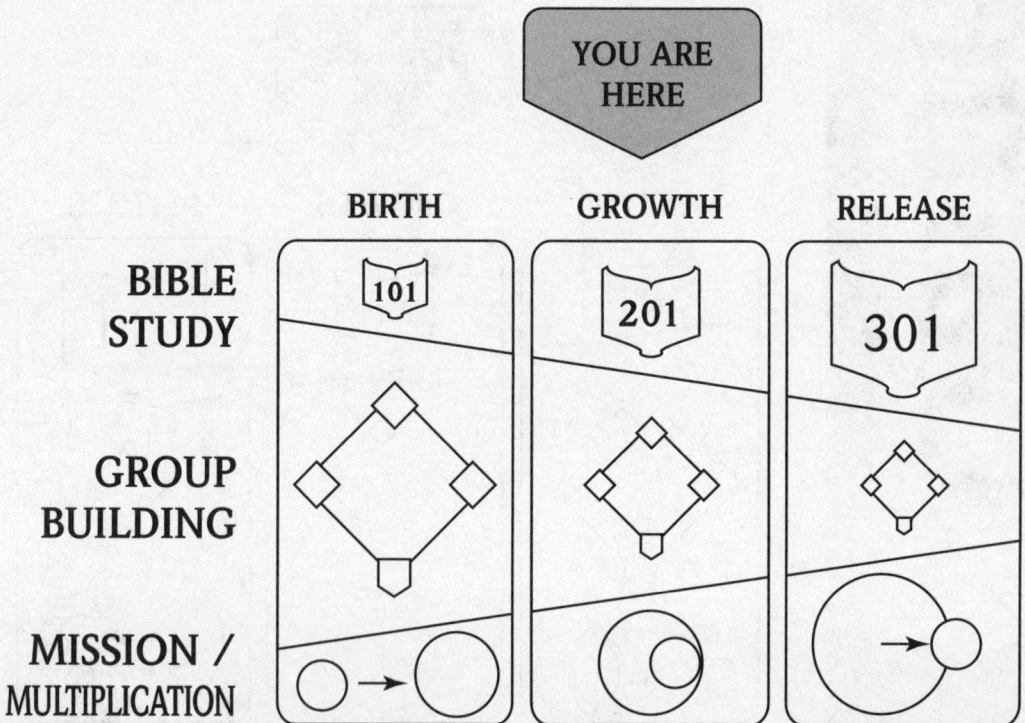

YOU ARE HERE

	BIRTH	GROWTH	RELEASE
BIBLE STUDY	101	201	301
GROUP BUILDING			
MISSION / MULTIPLICATION			

The three essentials in a healthy small group are Bible Study, Group Building and Mission / Multiplication. You need all three to stay balanced—like a 3-legged stool.
- To focus only on Bible Study will lead to scholasticism.
- To focus only on Group Building will lead to narcissism.
- To focus only on Mission will lead to burnout.

You need a game plan for the life cycle of the group where all of these elements are present in a purpose-driven strategy.

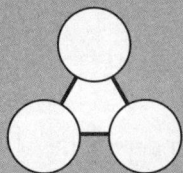

The 3-Legged Stool

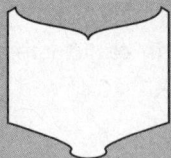

Bible Study

To dig into Scripture as a group.

Group Bible Study is quite different from individual Bible Study. The guided discussion questions are open-ended. And for those with little Bible background, there are reference notes to bring this person up to speed.

Group Building

To transform your group into a mission-driven team.

The nine basic needs of a group will be assigned to nine different people. Everyone has a job to fill, and when everyone is doing their job the group will grow spiritually and numerically. When new people enter the group, there is a selection of ICE-BREAKERS to start off the meeting and let the new people get acquainted.

Mission / Multiplication

To identify the Apprentice / Leader for birthing a new group.

In this stage, you will start dreaming about the possibility of starting a new group down the road. The questions at the close of each session will lead you carefully through the dreaming process—to help you discover an Apprentice / Leader who will eventually be the leader of a new group. This is an exciting challenge!

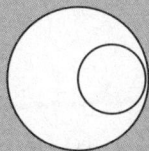

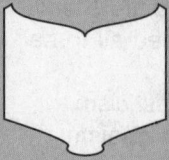

Bible Study

What is unique about Serendipity Group Bible Study?

Bible Study for groups is based on six principles. Principle 1: Level the playing field so that everyone can share—those who know the Bible and those who do not know the Bible. Principle 2: Share your spiritual story and let the people in your group get to know you. Principle 3: Ask open-ended questions that have no right or wrong answers. Principle 4: Keep a tight agenda. Principle 5: Subdivide into smaller groups so that everyone can participate. Principle 6: Affirm One Another—"Thanks for sharing."

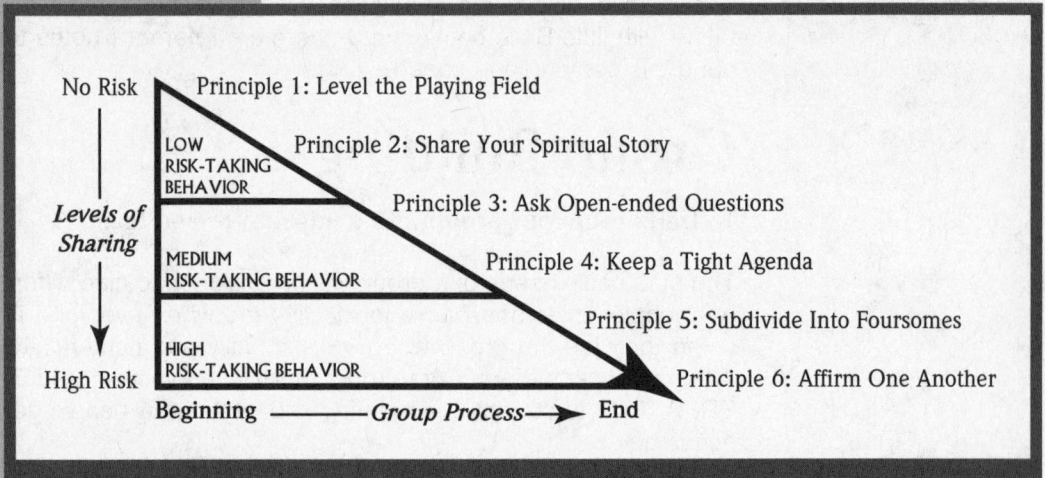

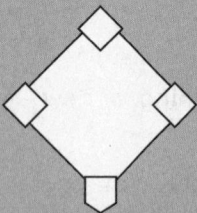

Group Building

What are the jobs that are needed on your team roster?

In the first or second session of this course, you need to fill out the roster on the next page. Then check every few weeks to see that everyone is "playing their position." If you do not have nine people in your group, you can double up on jobs until new people join your group and are assigned a job.

Your Small Group Team Roster

Mission Leader
(Left Field)
Keeps group focused on the mission to invite new people and eventually give birth to a new group. This person needs to be passionate and have a long-term perspective.

_____

Host
(Center Field)
Environmental engineer in charge of meeting location. Always on the lookout for moving to a new meeting location where new people will feel the "home field advantage."

_____

Social Leader
(Right Field)
Designates who is going to bring refreshments. Plans a party every month or so where new people are invited to visit and children are welcome.

_____

Caretaker
(Shortstop)
Takes new members under their wing. Makes sure they get acquainted. Always has an extra book, name tags and a list of group members and phone numbers.

_____

Bible Study Leader
(Second Base)
Takes over in the Bible Study time (30 minutes). Follows the agenda. Keeps the group moving. This person must be very time-conscious.

_____

Group Leader
(Pitcher)
Puts ball in play. Team encourager. Motivator. Sees to it that everyone is involved in the team effort.

_____

Caring Time Leader
(Third Base)
Takes over in the Caring Time. Records prayer requests and follows up on any prayer needs during the week. This person is the "heart" of the group.

_____

Worship Leader
(First Base)
Starts the meeting with singing and prayer. If a new person comes, shifts immediately to an ice-breaker to get acquainted, before the opening prayer.

_____

Apprentice / Leader
(Catcher)
The other half of the battery. Observes the infield. Calls "time" to discuss strategy and regroup. Stays focused.

_____

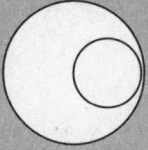

Mission / Multiplication

Where are you in the 3-stage life cycle of your mission?

You can't sit on a one-legged stool—or even a two-legged stool. It takes all three. The same is true of a small group; you need all three legs. A Bible Study and Care Group will eventually fall if it does not have a mission.

The mission goal is to eventually give birth to a new group. In this 201 course, the goals are: 1) to keep inviting new people to join your group and 2) to discover the Apprentice / Leader and leadership core for starting a new group down the road.

When a new person comes to the group, start off the meeting with one of the ice-breakers on the following pages. These ice-breakers are designed to be fun and easy to share, but they have a very important purpose—that is, to let the new person get acquainted with the group and share their spiritual story with the group, and hear the spiritual stories of those in the group.

YOU ARE HERE

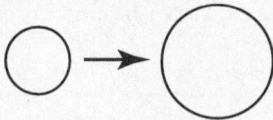

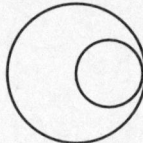

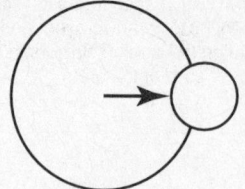

Stage 1	Stage 2	Stage 3
Growing your group size: **Desire**	Apprentice / Leader for new group: **Pregnancy**	Releasing the new cell / core: **Birth**

Ice-Breakers

I Am Somebody Who ...

Rotate around the group, one person reading the first item, the next person reading the second item, etc. Before answering, let everyone in the group try to GUESS what the answer would be: "Yes" ... "No" ... or "Maybe." After everyone has guessed, explain the answer. Anyone who guessed right gets $10. When every item on the list has been read, the person with the most "money" WINS.

I AM SOMEBODY WHO ...

Y N M
- ❏ ❏ ❏ would go on a blind date
- ❏ ❏ ❏ sings in the shower
- ❏ ❏ ❏ listens to music full blast
- ❏ ❏ ❏ likes to dance
- ❏ ❏ ❏ cries at movies
- ❏ ❏ ❏ stops to smell the flowers
- ❏ ❏ ❏ daydreams a lot
- ❏ ❏ ❏ likes to play practical jokes
- ❏ ❏ ❏ makes a "to do" list
- ❏ ❏ ❏ loves liver
- ❏ ❏ ❏ won't use a portable toilet
- ❏ ❏ ❏ likes thunderstorms
- ❏ ❏ ❏ enjoys romance novels
- ❏ ❏ ❏ loves crossword puzzles
- ❏ ❏ ❏ hates flying
- ❏ ❏ ❏ fixes my own car

Y N M
- ❏ ❏ ❏ would enjoy skydiving
- ❏ ❏ ❏ has a black belt in karate
- ❏ ❏ ❏ watches soap operas
- ❏ ❏ ❏ is afraid of the dark
- ❏ ❏ ❏ goes to bed early
- ❏ ❏ ❏ plays the guitar
- ❏ ❏ ❏ talks to plants
- ❏ ❏ ❏ will ask a stranger for directions
- ❏ ❏ ❏ sleeps until the last second
- ❏ ❏ ❏ likes to travel alone
- ❏ ❏ ❏ reads the financial page
- ❏ ❏ ❏ saves for a rainy day
- ❏ ❏ ❏ lies about my age
- ❏ ❏ ❏ yells at the umpire
- ❏ ❏ ❏ closes my eyes during scary movies

Press Conference

This is a great activity for a new group or when new people are joining an established group. Interview one person with these questions.

1. What is your nickname and how did you get it?

2. Where did you grow up? Where was the "watering hole" in your hometown—where kids got together?

3. What did you do for kicks then? What about now?

4. What was the turning point in your spiritual life?

5. What prompted you to come to this group?

6. What do you want to get out of this group?

Down Memory Lane

Celebrate the childhood memories of the way you were. Choose one or more of the topics listed below and answer the question related to it. If time allows, do another round.

HOME SWEET HOME–What do you remember about your childhood home?

TELEVISION—What was your favorite TV program or radio show?

OLD SCHOOLHOUSE—What were your best and worst subjects in school?

LIBRARY—What did you like to read (and where)?

TELEPHONE—How much time did you spend on the phone each day?

MOVIES—Who was your favorite movie star?

CASH FLOW—What did you do for spending money?

SPORTS—What was your favorite sport or team?

GRANDPA'S HOUSE—Where did your grandparents live? When did you visit them?

POLICE—Did you ever get in trouble with the law?

WEEKENDS—What was the thing to do on Saturday night?

Wallet Scavenger Hunt

With your wallet or purse, use the set of questions below. You get two minutes in silence to go through your possessions and find these items. Then break the silence and "show-and-tell" what you have chosen. For instance, "The thing I have had for the longest time is ... this picture of me when I was a baby."

1. The thing I have had for the LONGEST TIME in my wallet is ...

2. The thing that has SENTIMENTAL VALUE is ...

3. The thing that reminds me of a FUN TIME is ...

4. The most REVEALING thing about me in my wallet is ...

The Grand Total

This is a fun ice-breaker that has additional uses. You can use this ice-breaker to divide your group into two subgroups (odds and evens). You can also calculate who has the highest and lowest totals if you need a fun way to select someone to do a particular task, such as bring refreshments or be first to tell their story.

Fill each box with the correct number and then total your score. When everyone is finished, go around the group and explain how you got your total.

☐	X	☐	=	☐
Number of hours you sleep		Number of miles you walk daily		Subtotal

☐ X ☐ = ☐

Number of hours   Number of miles   Subtotal
you sleep   you walk daily

☐ — ☐ = ☐

Number of speeding   Number of times sent   Subtotal
tickets you've   to principal's office
received

☐ ÷ ☐ = ☐

Number of books you   Number of hours spent Subtotal
read this year for fun watching TV daily

☐ + ☐ = ☐

Number of push-ups   Number of pounds   Subtotal
you can do   you lost this year

☐

GRAND
TOTAL

Find Yourself in the Picture

In this drawing, which child do you identify with—or which one best portrays you right now? Share with your group which child you would choose and why. You can also use this as an affirmation exercise, by assigning each person in your group to a child in the picture.

Four Facts, One Lie

Everyone in the group should answer the following five questions. One of the five answers should be a lie! The rest of the group members can guess which of your answers is a lie.

1. At age 7, my favorite TV show was ...

2. At age 9, my hero was ...

3. At age 11, I wanted to be a ...

4. At age 13, my favorite music was ...

5. Right now, my favorite pastime is ...

Old-Fashioned Auction

Just like an old-fashioned auction, conduct an out loud auction in your group—starting each item at $50. Everybody starts out with $1,000. Select an auctioneer. This person can also get in on the bidding. Remember, start the bidding on each item at $50. Then, write the winning bid in the left column and the winner's name in the right column. Remember, you only have $1,000 to spend for the whole game. AUCTIONEER: Start off by asking, "Who will give me $50 for a 1965 red MG convertible?" ... and keep going until you have a winner. Keep this auction to 10 minutes.

WINNING BID   WINNER

$_____ 1965 red MG convertible in perfect condition   _____

$_____ Winter vacation in Hawaii for two   _____

$_____ Two Super Bowl tickets on the 50-yard line   _____

$_____ One year of no hassles with my kids / parents   _____

$_____ Holy Land tour hosted by my favorite Christian _____
                 leader

$_____ Season pass to ski resort of my choice   _____

$_____ Two months off to do anything I want, with pay _____

$_____ Home theater with surround sound   _____

$_____ Breakfast in bed for one year   _____

$_____ Two front-row tickets at the concert of my choice _____

$_____ Two-week Caribbean cruise with my spouse in   _____
                 honeymoon suite

$_____ Shopping spree at Saks Fifth Avenue   _____

$_____ Six months of maid service   _____

$_____ All-expense-paid family vacation to Disney World_____

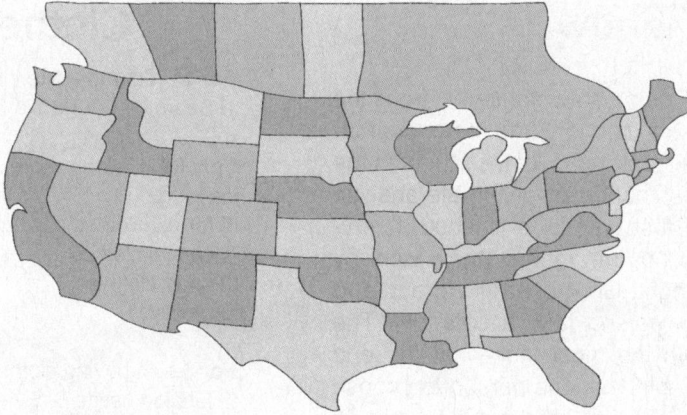

Places in My Life

On the map above, put six dots to indicate these significant places in your journey. Then go around and have each person explain the dots:

- the place where I was born
- the place where I spent most of my life
- the place where I first fell in love
- the place where I went or would like to go on a honeymoon
- the place where God first became real to me
- the place where I would like to retire

The Four Quaker Questions

This is an old Quaker activity which Serendipity has adapted over the years. Go around the group and share your answers to the questions, everyone answering #1. Then, everyone answers #2, etc. This ice-breaker has been known to take between 30 and 60 minutes for some groups.

1. Where were you living between the ages of 7 and 12, and what were the winters like then?

2. How was your home heated during that time?

3. What was the center of warmth in your life when you were a child? (It could be a place in the house, a time of year, a person, etc.)

4. When did God become a "warm" person to you ... and how did it happen?

KWIZ Show

Like a TV quiz show, someone from the group picks a category and reads the four questions—pausing to let the others in the group guess before revealing the answer. When the first person is finished, everyone adds up the money they won by guessing right. Go around the group and have each person take a category. The person with the most money at the end wins. To begin, ask one person to choose a CATEGORY and read out loud the $1 question. Before answering, let everyone try to GUESS the answer. When everyone has guessed, the person answers the question, and anyone who guessed right puts $1 in the margin, etc. until the first person has read all four questions in the CATEGORY.

Clothes

For $1: I'm more likely to shop at:
❑ Sears   ❑ Saks Fifth Avenue

For $2: I feel more comfortable wearing:
❑ formal clothes
❑ casual clothes
❑ sport clothes
❑ grubbies

For $3: In buying clothes, I look for:
❑ fashion / style
❑ price
❑ name brand
❑ quality

For $4: In buying clothes, I usually:
❑ shop all day for a bargain
❑ go to one store, but try on everything
❑ buy the first thing I try on
❑ buy without trying it on

Tastes

For $1: In music, I am closer to:
❑ Bach   ❑ Beatles

For $2: In furniture, I prefer:
❑ Early American
❑ French Provincial
❑ Scandinavian—contemporary
❑ Hodgepodge—little of everything

For $3: My choice of reading material is:
❑ science fiction   ❑ sports
❑ mystery   ❑ romance

For $4: If I had $1,000 to splurge, I would buy:
❑ one original painting
❑ two numbered prints
❑ three reproductions and an easy chair
❑ four cheap imitations, easy chair and color TV

Travel

For $1: For travel, I prefer:
❑ excitement   ❑ enrichment

For $2: On a vacation, my lifestyle is:
❑ go-go all the time
❑ slow and easy
❑ party every night and sleep in

For $3: In packing for a trip, I include:
❑ toothbrush and change of underwear
❑ light bag and good book
❑ small suitcase and nice outfit
❑ all but the kitchen sink

For $4: If I had money to blow, I would choose:
❑ one glorious night in a luxury hotel
❑ a weekend in a nice hotel
❑ a full week in a cheap motel
❑ two weeks camping in the boondocks

Habits

For $1: I am more likely to squeeze the toothpaste:
❒ in the middle   ❒ from the end

For $2: If I am lost, I will probably:
❒ stop and ask directions
❒ check the map
❒ find the way by driving around

For $3: I read the newspaper starting with the:
❒ front page
❒ funnies
❒ sports
❒ entertainment section

For $4: When I undress at night, I put my clothes:
❒ on a hanger in the closet
❒ folded neatly over a chair
❒ into a hamper or clothes basket
❒ on the floor

Shows

For $1: I am more likely to:
❒ go see a first-run movie
❒ rent a video at home

For $2: On TV, my first choice is:
❒ news
❒ sports
❒ sitcoms

For $3: If a show gets scary, I will usually:
❒ go to the restroom
❒ close my eyes
❒ clutch a friend
❒ love it

For $4: In movies, I prefer:
❒ romantic comedies
❒ serious drama
❒ action films
❒ Disney animation

Food

For $1: I prefer to eat at a:
❒ fast-food restaurant
❒ fancy restaurant

For $2: On the menu, I look for something:
❒ familiar
❒ different
❒ way-out

For $3: When eating chicken, my preference is a:
❒ drumstick
❒ wing
❒ breast
❒ gizzard

For $4: I draw the line when it comes to eating:
❒ frog legs
❒ snails
❒ raw oysters
❒ Rocky Mountain oysters

Work

For $1: I prefer to work at a job that is:
❒ too big to handle
❒ too small to be challenging

For $2: The job I find most unpleasant is:
❒ cleaning the house
❒ working in the yard
❒ balancing the checkbook

For $3: In choosing a job, I look for:
❒ salary
❒ security
❒ fulfillment
❒ working conditions

For $4: If I had to choose between these jobs, I would choose:
❒ pickle inspector at processing plant
❒ complaint officer at department store
❒ bedpan changer at hospital
❒ personnel manager in charge of firing

Let Me Tell You About My Day

What was your day like today? Use one of the characters below to help you describe your day to the group. Feel free to elaborate.

GREEK TRAGEDY
It was classic, not a dry eye in the house.

SOAP OPERA
I didn't think these things could happen, until it happened to me.

EPISODE OF THREE STOOGES
I was Larry, trapped between Curly and Moe.

ACTION ADVENTURE
When I rode onto the scene, everybody noticed.

LATE NIGHT NEWS
It might as well have been broadcast over the airwaves.

BIBLE EPIC
Cecil B. DeMille couldn't have done it any better.

BORING LECTURE
The biggest challenge of the day was staying awake.

FIREWORKS DISPLAY
It was spectacular.

PROFESSIONAL WRESTLING MATCH
I feel as if Hulk Hogan's been coming after me.

Music in My Life

Put an *"X"* on each of the lines below—somewhere between the two extremes—to indicate how you are feeling right now about each area of your life. If time is limited, choose only two or three:

IN MY PERSONAL LIFE, I'M FEELING LIKE ...
Blues in the Night_____ **Feeling Groovy**

IN MY FAMILY LIFE, I'M FEELING LIKE ...
Stormy Weather _____ **The Sound of Music**

IN MY EMOTIONAL LIFE, I'M FEELING LIKE ...
The Feeling Is Gone _____ **On Eagle's Wings**

IN MY WORK, SCHOOL OR CAREER, I'M FEELING LIKE ...
Take This Job and Shove It _____ **The Future's So Bright I Gotta Wear Shades**

IN MY SPIRITUAL LIFE, I'M FEELING LIKE ...
Sounds of Silence _____ **Hallelujah Chorus**

My Childhood Table

Try to recall the table where you ate most of your meals as a child, and the people who sat around that table. Use the questions below to describe these significant relationships, and how they helped to shape the person you are today.

1. What was the shape of the table?
2. Where did you sit?
3. Who else was at the table?
4. If you had to describe each person with a color, what would be the color of (for instance):
   ❐ Your father? (e.g., dark blue, because he was conservative like IBM)
   ❐ Your mother? (e.g., light green, because she reminded me of springtime)
5. If you had to describe the atmosphere at the table with a color, what would you choose? (e.g., bright orange, because it was warm and light)
6. Who was the person at the table who praised you and made you feel special?
7. Who provided the spiritual leadership in your home?

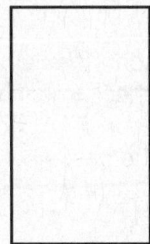

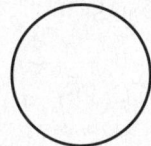

Home Improvement

Take inventory of your own life. Bob Munger, in his booklet *My Heart—Christ's Home*, describes the areas of a person's life as the rooms of a house. Give yourself a grade on each room as follows, then share with the others your best and worst grade.

❐ A = excellent   ❐ C = passing, needs a little dusting
❐ B = good   ❐ D = passing, but needs a lot of improvement

LIBRARY: This room is in your mind—what you allow to go into it and come out of it. It is the "control room" of the entire house.

DINING ROOM: Appetites, desires; those things your mind and spirit feed on for nourishment.

DRAWING ROOM: This is where you draw close to God—seeking time with him daily, not just in times of distress or need.

WORKSHOP: This room is where your gifts, talents and skills are put to work for God—by the power of the Spirit.

RUMPUS ROOM: The social area of your life; the things you do to amuse yourself and others.

HALL CLOSET: The one secret place that no one knows about, but is a real stumbling block in your walk in the Spirit.

How Is It With Your Soul?

John Wesley, the founder of the Methodist Church, asked his "class meetings" to check in each week at their small group meeting with this question: "How is it with your soul?" To answer this question, choose one of these four allegories to explain the past week in your life:

WEATHER: For example: "This week has been mostly cloudy, with some thunderstorms at midweek. Right now, the weather is a little brighter ..."

MUSIC: For example: "This past week has been like heavy rock music—almost too loud. The sound seems to reverberate off the walls."

COLOR: For example: "This past week has been mostly fall colors—deep orange, flaming red and pumpkin."

SEASON
OF THE   For example: "This past week has been like springtime. New signs of
YEAR: life are beginning to appear on the barren trees, and a few shoots of winter wheat are breaking through the frozen ground."

My Spiritual Journey

The half-finished sentences below are designed to help you share your spiritual story. Ask one person to finish all the sentences. Then move to the next person, etc. If you are short on time, have only one person tell their story in this session.

1. RELIGIOUS BACKGROUND: My spiritual story begins in my home as a child, where the religious training was ...

2. CHURCH: The church that I went to as a child was ...

3. SIGNIFICANT PERSON: The person who had the greatest influence on my spiritual formation was ...

4. PERSONAL ENCOUNTER: The first time God became more than just a name to me was when ...

5. JOURNEY: Since my personal encounter with God, my Christian life might be described as ...

6. PRESENT: On a scale from 1 to 10, I would describe my spiritual energy level right now as a ...

7. NEXT STEP: The thing I need to work on right now in my spiritual life is ...

Bragging Rights

Check your group for bragging rights in these categories.

❐ SPEEDING TICKETS: the person with the most speeding tickets
❐ BROKEN BONES: the person with the most broken bones
❐ STITCHES: the person with the most stitches
❐ SCARS: the person with the longest scar
❐ FISH OR GAME: the person who claims they caught the largest fish or killed the largest animal
❐ STUNTS: the person with the most death-defying story
❐ IRON: the person who can pump the most iron

Personal Habits

Go around and have everyone in your group finish the sentence on the first category by putting an "**X**" somewhere between the two extremes. (For instance, on HOUSE-WORK ... I would put myself closer to "Where's the floor?")

ON HOUSEWORK, I AM SOMEWHERE BETWEEN:
Eat off the floor_____Where's the floor?

ON COOKING, I AM SOMEWHERE BETWEEN:
Every meal is an act of worship_____Make it fast and hold the frills

ON EXERCISING, I AM SOMEWHERE BETWEEN:
Workout every morning_____Click the remote

ON SHOPPING, I AM SOMEWHERE BETWEEN:
Shop all day for a bargain_____Only the best

ON EATING, I AM SOMEWHERE BETWEEN:
You are what you eat_____Eat, drink and be merry

American Graffiti

If Hollywood made a movie about your life on the night of your high school prom, what would be needed? Let each person in your group have a few minutes to recall these details. If you have more than four or five in your group, ask everyone to choose two or three topics to talk about.

1. LOCATION: Where were you living?
2. WEIGHT: How much did you weigh—soaking wet?
3. PROM: Where was it held?
4. DATE: Who did you take?
5. CAR / TRANSPORTATION: How did you get there?
   (If you used a car, what was the model, year, color, condition?)
6. ATTIRE: What did you wear?
7. PROGRAM: What was the entertainment?
8. AFTERWARD: What did you do afterward?
9. HIGHLIGHT: What was the highlight of the evening?
10. HOMECOMING: If you could go back and visit your high school, who would you like to see?

Group Orchestra

Read out loud the first item and let everyone nominate the person in your group for this musical instrument in your group orchestra. Then, read aloud the next instrument, and call out another name, etc.

ANGELIC HARP: Soft, gentle, melodious, wooing with heavenly sounds.

OLD-FASHIONED WASHBOARD: Nonconforming, childlike and fun.

PLAYER PIANO: Mischievous, raucous, honky-tonk—delightfully carefree.

KETTLEDRUM: Strong, vibrant, commanding when needed but usually in the background.

PASSIONATE CASTANET: Full of Spanish fervor—intense and always upbeat.

STRADIVARIUS VIOLIN: Priceless, exquisite, soul-piercing—with the touch of the master.

FLUTTERING FLUTE: Tender, lighthearted, wide-ranging and clear as crystal.

SCOTTISH BAGPIPES: Forthright, distinctive and unmistakable.

SQUARE DANCE FIDDLE: Folksy, down-to-earth, toe-tapping—sprightly and full of energy.

ENCHANTING OBOE: Haunting, charming, disarming—even the cobra is harmless with this sound.

MELLOW CELLO: Deep, sonorous, compassionate—adding body and depth to the orchestra.

PIPE ORGAN: Grand, magnificent, rich—versatile and commanding.

HERALDING TRUMPET: Stirring, lively, invigorating—signaling attention and attack.

CLASSICAL GUITAR: Contemplative, profound, thoughtful *and* thought-provoking.

ONE-MAN BAND: Able to do many things well, all at once.

COMB AND TISSUE PAPER: Makeshift, original, uncomplicated—homespun and creative.

SWINGING TROMBONE: Warm, rich—great in solo or background support.

Broadway Show

Imagine for a moment that your group has been chosen to produce a Broadway show, and you had to choose people from your group for all of the jobs for this production. Have someone read out loud the job description for the first job below—PRODUCER. Then, let everyone in your group call out the name of the person in your group who would best fit this job. (You don't have to agree.) Then read the job description for the next job and let everyone nominate another person, etc. You only have 10 minutes for this assignment, so move fast.

PRODUCER: Typical Hollywood business tycoon; extravagant, big-budget, big-production magnate in the Steven Spielberg style.

DIRECTOR: Creative, imaginative brains who coordinates the production and draws the best out of others.

HEROINE: Beautiful, captivating, everybody's heart throb; defenseless when men are around, but nobody's fool.

HERO: Tough, macho, champion of the underdog, knight in shining armor; defender of truth.

COMEDIAN: Childlike, happy-go-lucky, outrageously funny, keeps everyone laughing.

CHARACTER PERSON: Rugged individualist, outrageously different, colorful, adds spice to any surrounding.

FALL GUY: Easy-going, nonchalant character who wins the hearts of everyone by being the "foil" of the heavy characters.

TECHNICAL DIRECTOR: The genius for "sound and lights"; creates the perfect atmosphere.

COMPOSER OF LYRICS: Communicates in music what everybody understands; heavy into feelings, moods, outbursts of energy.

PUBLICITY AGENT: Advertising and public relations expert; knows all the angles, good at one-liners, a flair for "hot" news.

VILLAIN: The "bad guy" who really is the heavy for the plot, forces others to think, challenges traditional values; out to destroy anything artificial or hypocritical.

AUTHOR: Shy, aloof; very much in touch with feelings, sensitive to people, puts into words what others only feel.

STAGEHAND: Supportive, behind-the-scenes person who makes things run smoothly; patient and tolerant.

Wild Predictions

Try to match the people in your group to the crazy forecasts below. (Don't take it too seriously; it's meant to be fun!) Read out loud the first item and ask everyone to call out the name of the person who is most likely to accomplish this feat. Then, read the next item and ask everyone to make a new prediction, etc.

THE PERSON IN OUR GROUP MOST LIKELY TO ...

Be the used-car salesperson of the year

Replace Regis Philbin on *Regis and Kathie Lee*

Replace Vanna White on *Wheel of Fortune*

Rollerblade across the country

Open a charm school for Harley-Davidson bikers

Discover a new use for underarm deodorant

Run a dating service for lonely singles

Rise to the top in the CIA

Appear on the cover of *Muscle & Fitness Magazine*

Win the Iditarod dogsled race in Alaska

Make a fortune on pay toilet rentals

Write a best-selling novel based on their love life

Get listed in the *Guinness Book of World Records* for marathon dancing

Win the blue ribbon at the state fair for best Rocky Mountain oyster recipe

Bungee jump off the Golden Gate Bridge

Be the first woman to win the Indianapolis 500

Win the *MAD Magazine* award for worst jokes

Career Placements

Read the list of career choices aloud and quickly choose someone in your group for each job—based upon their unique gifts and talents. Have fun!

SPACE ENVIRONMENTAL ENGINEER: in charge of designing the bathrooms on space shuttles

SCHOOL BUS DRIVER: for junior high kids in New York City (earplugs supplied)

WRITER: of an "advice to the lovelorn" column in Hollywood

SUPERVISOR: of a complaint department for a large automobile dealership and service department

ANIMAL PSYCHIATRIST: for French poodles in a fashionable suburb of Paris

RESEARCH SCIENTIST: studying the fertilization patterns of the dodo bird—now extinct

SAFARI GUIDE: in the heart of Africa—for wealthy widows and eccentric bachelors

LITTLE LEAGUE BASEBALL COACH: in Mudville, Illinois—last year's record was 0 and 12

MANAGER: of your local McDonald's during the holiday rush with 210 teenage employees

LIBRARIAN: for the Walt Disney Hall of Fame memorabilia

CHOREOGRAPHER: for the Dallas Cowboys cheerleaders

NURSE'S AIDE: at a home for retired Sumo wrestlers

SECURITY GUARD: crowd control officer at a rock concert

ORGANIZER: of paperwork for Congress

PUBLIC RELATIONS MANAGER: for Dennis Rodman

BODYGUARD: for Rush Limbaugh on a speaking tour of feminist groups

TOY ASSEMBLY PERSON: for a toy store over the holidays

You and Me, Partner

Think of the people in your group as you read over the list of activities below. If you had to choose someone from your group to be your partner, who would you choose to do these activities with? Jot down each person's name beside the activity. You can use each person's name only once and you have to use everyone's name once—so think it through before you jot down their names. Then, let one person listen to what others chose for them. Then, move to the next person, etc., around your group.

WHO WOULD YOU CHOOSE FOR THE FOLLOWING?

_____ ENDURANCE DANCE CONTEST partner

_____ BOBSLED RACE partner for the Olympics

_____ TRAPEZE ACT partner

_____ MY UNDERSTUDY for my debut in a Broadway musical

_____ BEST MAN or MAID OF HONOR at my wedding

_____ SECRET UNDERCOVER AGENT copartner

_____ BODYGUARD for me when I strike it rich

_____ MOUNTAIN CLIMBING partner in climbing Mt. Everest

_____ ASTRONAUT to fly the space shuttle while I walk in space

_____ SAND CASTLE TOURNAMENT building partner

_____ PIT CREW foreman for entry in Indianapolis 500

_____ AUTHOR for my biography

_____ SURGEON to operate on me for a life-threatening cancer

_____ NEW BUSINESS START-UP partner

_____ TAG-TEAM partner for a professional wrestling match

_____ HEAVY-DUTY PRAYER partner

My Gourmet Group

Here's a chance to pass out some much deserved praise for the people who have made your group something special. Ask one person to sit in silence while the others explain the delicacy you would choose to describe the contribution this person has made to your group. Repeat the process for each member of the group.

CAVIAR: That special touch of class and aristocratic taste that has made the rest of us feel like royalty.

PRIME RIB: Stable, brawny, macho, the generous mainstay of any menu; juicy, mouth-watering "perfect cut" for good nourishment.

IMPORTED CHEESE: Distinctive, tangy, mellow with age; adds depth to any meal.

VINEGAR AND OIL: Tart, witty, dry; a rare combination of healing ointment and pungent spice to add "bite" to the salad.

ARTICHOKE HEARTS: Tender and disarmingly vulnerable; whets the appetite for heartfelt sharing.

FRENCH PASTRY: Tempting, irresistible "creme de la creme" dessert; the connoisseur's delight for topping off a meal.

PHEASANT UNDER GLASS: Wild, totally unique, a rare dish for people who appreciate original fare.

CARAFE OF WINE: Sparkling, effervescent, exuberant and joyful; outrageously free and liberating to the rest of us.

ESCARGOT AND OYSTERS: Priceless treasures of the sea once out of their shells; succulent, delicate and irreplaceable.

FRESH FRUIT: Vine-ripened, energy-filled, invigorating; the perfect treat after a heavy meal.

ITALIAN ICE CREAMS: Colorful, flavorful, delightfully childlike; the unexpected surprise in our group.

Thank You

How would you describe your experience with this group? Choose one of the animals below that best describes how your experience in this group affected your life. Then share your responses with the group.

WILD EAGLE: You have helped to heal my wings, and taught me how to soar again.

TOWERING GIRAFFE: You have helped me to hold my head up and stick my neck out, and reach over the fences I have built.

PLAYFUL PORPOISE: You have helped me to find a new freedom and a whole new world to play in.

COLORFUL PEACOCK: You have told me that I'm beautiful; I've started to believe it, and it's changing my life.

SAFARI ELEPHANT: I have enjoyed this new adventure, and I'm not going to forget it, or this group; I can hardly wait for the next safari.

LOVABLE HIPPOPOTAMUS: You have let me surface and bask in the warm sunshine of God's love.

LANKY LEOPARD: You have helped me to look closely at myself and see some spots, and you still accept me the way I am.

DANCING BEAR: You have taught me to dance in the midst of pain, and you have helped me to reach out and hug again.

ALL-WEATHER DUCK: You have helped me to celebrate life—even in stormy weather—and to sing in the rain.

Academy Awards

You have had a chance to observe the gifts and talents of the members of your group. Now you will have a chance to pass out some much deserved praise for the contribution that each member of the group has made to your life. Read out loud the first award. Then let everyone nominate the person they feel is the most deserving for that award. Then read the next award, etc., through the list. Have fun!

SPARK PLUG AWARD: for the person who ignited the group

DEAR ABBY AWARD: for the person who cared enough to listen

ROYAL GIRDLE AWARD: for the person who supported us

WINNIE THE POOH AWARD: for the warm, caring person when someone needed a hug

ROCK OF GIBRALTER AWARD: for the person who was strong in the tough times of our group

OPRAH AWARD: for the person who asked the fun questions that got us to talk

TED KOPPEL AWARD: for the person who asked the heavy questions that made us think

KING ARTHUR'S AWARD: for the knight in shining armor

PINK PANTHER AWARD: for the detective who made us deal with Scripture

NOBEL PEACE PRIZE: for the person who harmonized our differences of opinion without diminishing anyone

BIG MAC AWARD: for the person who showed the biggest hunger for spiritual things

SERENDIPITY CROWN: for the person who grew the most spiritually during the course—in your estimation

You Remind Me of Jesus

Every Christian reflects the character of Jesus in some way. As your group has gotten to know each other, you can begin to see how each person demonstrates Christ in their very own personality. Go around the circle and have each person listen while others take turns telling that person what they notice in him or her that reminds them of Jesus. You may also want to tell them why you selected what you did.

YOU REMIND ME OF ...

JESUS THE HEALER: You seem to be able to touch someone's life with your compassion and help make them whole.

JESUS THE SERVANT: There's nothing that you wouldn't do for someone.

JESUS THE PREACHER: You share your faith in a way that challenges and inspires people.

JESUS THE LEADER: As Jesus had a plan for the disciples, you are able to lead others in a way that honors God.

JESUS THE REBEL: By doing the unexpected, you remind me of Jesus' way of revealing God in unique, surprising ways.

JESUS THE RECONCILER: Like Jesus, you have the ability to be a peacemaker between others.

JESUS THE TEACHER: You have a gift for bringing light and understanding to God's Word.

JESUS THE CRITIC: You have the courage to say what needs to be said, even if it isn't always popular.

JESUS THE SACRIFICE: Like Jesus, you seem willing to sacrifice anything to glorify God.

Reflections

Take some time to evaluate the life of your group by using the statements below. Read the first sentence out loud and ask everyone to explain where they would put a dot between the two extremes. When you are finished, go back and give your group an overall grade in the category of Group Building, Bible Study and Mission.

◇ GROUP BUILDING

On celebrating life and having fun together, we were more like a ...
wet blanket _____ hot tub

On becoming a caring community, we were more like a ...
prickly pear _____ cuddly teddy bear

📖 BIBLE STUDY

On sharing our spiritual stories, we were more like a ...
shallow pond _____ spring-fed lake

On digging into Scripture, we were more like a ...
slow-moving snail _____ voracious anteater

◉ MISSION

On inviting new people into our group, we were more like a ...
barbed-wire fence _____ wide-open door

On stretching our vision for mission, we were more like an ...
ostrich _____ eagle

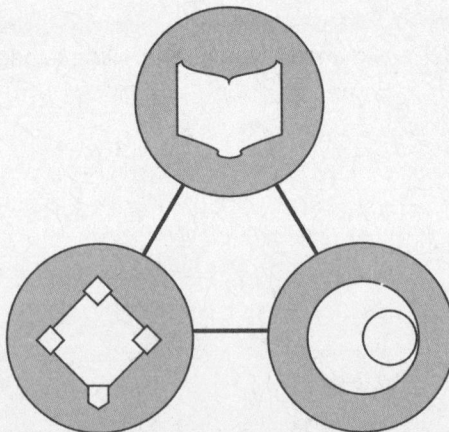

Human Bingo / Party Mixer

After the leader says "Go!" circulate the room, asking people the things described in the boxes. If someone answers "Yes" to a question, have them sign their initials in that box. Continue until someone completes the entire card—or one row if you don't have that much time. You can only use someone's name twice, and you cannot use your own name on your card.

can juggle	TP'd a house	never used an outhouse	sings in the shower	rec'd 6+ traffic tickets	paddled in school	watches Sesame Street
sleeps in church regularly	never changed a diaper	split pants in public	milked a cow	born out of the country	has been to Hawaii	can do the splits
watches soap operas	can touch tongue to nose	rode a motor-cycle	never ridden a horse	moved twice last year	sleeps on a waterbed	has hole in sock
walked in wrong restroom	loves classical music	skipped school	**FREE**	broke a leg	has a hot tub	loves eating sushi
is an only child	loves raw oysters	has a 3-inch + scar	doesn't wear PJ's	smoked a cigar	can dance the Charleston	weighs under 110 lbs.
likes writing poetry	still has tonsils	loves crossword puzzles	likes bubble baths	wearing Fruit of the Loom	doesn't use mouth-wash	often watches cartoons
kissed on first date	can wiggle ears	can play the guitar	plays chess regularly	reads the comics first	can touch palms to floor	sleeps with stuffed animal

Group Covenant

Any group can benefit from creating a group covenant. Reserve some time during one of the first meetings to discuss answers to the following questions. When everyone in the group has the same expectations for the group, everything runs more smoothly.

1. The purpose of our group is:

2. The goals of our group are:

3. We will meet for _____ weeks, after which we will decide if we wish to continue as a group. If we do decide to continue, we will reconsider this covenant.

4. We will meet _____ (weekly, every other week, monthly).

5. Our meetings will be from _____ o'clock to _____ o'clock, and we will strive to start and end on time.

6. We will meet at _____
   or rotate from house to house.

7. We will take care of the following details: ❐ child care   ❐ refreshments

8. We agree to the following rules for our group:

   ❐ PRIORITY: While we are in this group, group meetings have priority.

   ❐ PARTICIPATION: Everyone is given the right to their own opinion and all questions are respected.

   ❐ CONFIDENTIALITY: Anything said in the meeting is not to be repeated outside the meeting.

   ❐ EMPTY CHAIR: The group stays open to new people and invites prospective members to visit the group.

   ❐ SUPPORT: Permission is given to call each other in times of need.

   ❐ ADVICE GIVING: Unsolicited advice is not allowed.

   ❐ MISSION: We will do all that is in our power to start a new group.

9:24 *The girl is not dead but asleep.* Jesus does not mean by this that she has not really died but instead is in some sort of coma. The presence of the mourners and the laughter that greeted this statement all say the same thing: the child was truly dead. Jesus uses this same expression in reference to Lazarus, and he was clearly dead. His body had even begun to decompose (John 11:11–15). What he means is that she is not permanently dead.

9:26 *she got up.* Jesus raises her from the dead.

9:27–34 These next two stories not only continue to emphasize Jesus' miraculous ability to heal; but the giving of sight to the blind and speech to the mute are especially intended to be seen as signs that he is indeed the Messiah who has come to bring sight and speech to his people (Isa. 35:5–6; see also Matt. 11:2–6). Through Jesus, the time of God's redemption of his people has arrived.

9:27 *two blind men.* Blindness was common in the ancient world, often due to infection. Blindness was of various sorts. The most widespread condition was ophthalmia, a form of conjunctivitis that was highly contagious. It was transmitted by flies and was aggravated by the dust and glare of the arid Middle Eastern environment. Blindness also resulted from glaucoma and cataracts, and was sometimes present at birth.

Have mercy on us. Mercy is not as much an emotion as it is concrete aid.

Son of David. This is a clear messianic title, since there was a strong expectation based upon Old Testament prophecies that the Messiah would be a king in the line of David. The Messiah was understood to have the power to heal (see Matt. 11:4–5). In their cry for mercy, the blind men set the example for how people enter God's kingdom. They understand their need for God's help, and believe that in Jesus this help can be found.

9:29 *According to your faith.* As with the story of the woman (v. 14), faith in Christ is shown to be the key that provides access to God's gracious power. The point is that God delights to respond to those who place their hope in him. But God is not a genie, nor is faith the magic lamp that gets God to do what one wants.

> *Faith in Christ is shown to be the key that provides access to God's gracious power. The point is that God delights to respond to those who place their hope in him. But God is not a genie, nor is faith the magic lamp that gets God to do what one wants.*

9:30 Jesus continues to be concerned that his ministry of healing individuals will obscure his greater task, which is to save people from their sins (see Matt.1:21).

9:32–34 The fourth and final healing in this section is an exorcism which restores speech to a mute. It also functions to summarize the meaning of the miracles throughout Matthew 8–9. The miracles force people to make choices about Jesus. Either they are seen as signs that draw people to Jesus (v. 33), or they are viewed as fraudulent, leading people to take entrenched positions of hostility against him (v. 34).

9:32 The man's affliction is attributed to a demon (see also Matt. 12:22).

9:33 *mute.* This word can mean either deaf or dumb or both.

Nothing like this has ever been seen in Israel. At the end of the Sermon on the Mount, Matthew contrasted Jesus' teaching with that of the religious leaders (Matt. 7:28–29). Here he contrasts his healing power with theirs. In terms of both teaching and healing Jesus stands above and against the religious leaders.

9:34 The reaction of the Pharisees stands in sharp contrast to the reaction of the crowd in verse 33. They dismiss his healings by attributing them to Satan.

7 Jesus the Messiah—Mark 8:27–38

THREE-PART AGENDA

ICE-BREAKER
15 Minutes

BIBLE STUDY
30 Minutes

CARING TIME
15–45 Minutes

> *LEADER: Check page M7 in the center section for a good ice-breaker, particularly if you have a new person at this meeting. In the Caring Time, is everyone sharing and are prayer requests being followed up?*

TO BEGIN THE BIBLE STUDY TIME
(Choose 1 or 2)

1. What's your favorite TV game show or question-and-answer game?

2. If your closest friends were asked what one word best describes you, what might they say?

3. When you misbehaved as a child, what did your parents say that made you feel most ashamed of what you had done?

READ SCRIPTURE & DISCUSS
(If you don't have time for all the questions in this section, conclude the Bible Study [30 min.] by answering question #7.)

Jesus forces his disciples to wrestle with his true identity. The people believed that the Christ or Messiah would be a military hero. Jesus' words about his suffering, death and resurrection were the opposite of this view.

1. If you were asked to describe yourself, what would you say?

2. Why is the question "Who do you say I am?" (v. 29) so important?

Peter's Confession of Christ

27Jesus and his disciples went on to the villages around Caesarea Philippi. On the way he asked them, "Who do people say I am?"

28They replied, "Some say John the Baptist; others say Elijah; and still others, one of the prophets."

29"But what about you?" he asked. "Who do you say I am?"

Peter answered, "You are the Christ.a"

30Jesus warned them not to tell anyone about him.

Jesus Predicts His Death

31He then began to teach them that the Son of Man must suffer many things and be rejected by the elders, chief priests and teachers of the law, and that he must be killed and after three days rise again. 32He spoke plainly about this, and Peter took him aside and began to rebuke him.

33But when Jesus turned and looked at his disciples, he rebuked Peter. "Get behind me, Satan!" he said. "You do not have in mind the things of God, but the things of men."

34Then he called the crowd to him along with his disciples and said: "If anyone would come after me, he must deny himself and take up his cross and follow me. 35For whoever wants to save his lifeb will lose it, but whoever loses his life for me and for the gospel will save it. 36What good is it for a man to gain the whole world, yet forfeit his soul? 37Or what can a man give in exchange for his soul? 38If anyone is ashamed of me and my words in this adulterous and sinful generation, the Son of Man will be ashamed of him when he comes in his Father's glory with the holy angels."

a29 Or *Messiah*. "The Christ" (Greek) and "the Messiah" (Hebrew) both mean "the Anointed One."   b35 The Greek word means either *life* or *soul*; also in verse 36.

3. Who did the people of Jesus' day think he was (v. 28)? Who do people today say Jesus is? What about you, and how has your answer changed over time?

4. What four things does Jesus prophesy about himself in verses 31 and 32?

5. How did Peter go from "star pupil" (v. 29) to being in the doghouse (v. 33)?

6. According to verses 34–38, what is involved in being a follower of Christ?

7. How does your relationship with Christ affect how you live? In what area of ministry do you feel most called to follow Jesus?

CARING TIME

(Choose 1 or 2 of these questions before taking prayer requests and closing in prayer. Be sure to pray for the empty chair.)

1. It's not too late to have someone new come to this study. Who could you invite for next week?

2. What are you doing to grow in Christ?

3. How can the group pray for you this week?

Summary. This is a pivotal point in the Gospel of Mark. For the first time, after many incidents that demonstrate Jesus' authority over all types of forces, the disciples indicate that they recognize Jesus as the Messiah. However, they still have the wrong idea about the nature and role of the Messiah.

8:27 *Caesarea Philippi.* This was a beautiful city on the slopes of Mt. Hermon, 25 miles north of Bethsaida. It had once been called Balinas when it was a center for Baal worship. It was later called Panias, because it was said that the god Pan had his birth in a cave in the hill. This region was also where the River Jordan began—a river of great importance to the history of Israel. At the time when Jesus and his disciples visited there, up on the hill there was a white marble temple dedicated to the godhead of Caesar. It is in this place full of rich associations with pagan, Greek, Jewish and Roman religions that Jesus, the Galilean, asks his disciples if they understand that he is the Anointed One sent by God.

8:28 *Some say.* The people are not clear about just who Jesus is, but tend to see him as one who paves the way for the Messiah. Some (like Herod—Mark 6:16) think he is John the Baptist come back to life (see note on Matt. 3:13 in Session 2). Others think he is the prophet Elijah (1 Kings 17–2 Kings 2), considered to be one of the greatest prophets of Israel who would appear again one day as the forerunner of the Messiah (Mal. 4:5; Mark 9:11–13). Still others are not willing to say which prophet he is, only that he is a prophet who has a message from God.

8:29 *Who do you say I am?* This is the crucial question in Mark's Gospel. With it the author is not only telling the story of the disciples' growth in their faith, but he forces his readers to consider how they will answer the question as well.

Christ. Peter correctly identifies him as the Christ, the Greek term for the Hebrew word Messiah. See note on Luke 2:11 in Session 1.

8:30 *not to tell anyone.* Jesus urges them to be silent about what they know. While they know he is the Messiah, they do not yet know what kind of Messiah he is. This recognition of who Jesus is follows immediately after the strange two-stage healing of the blind man (Mark 8:22–26). The placement of this story indicates that the healing was meant to be an illustration of the disciples' growing under-

standing of who Jesus was. Like the blind man, the disciples received the "first touch" of healing. Their spiritual blindness, which, so far, prevented them from understanding Jesus, is beginning to be healed, but they are not yet totally restored to full sight—as the next incident shows (Mark 8:31–33).

8:31–38 Having discovered that Jesus is the Messiah, the disciples now need to know what kind of Messiah he is. He is not, as their culture led them to believe, a nationalistic hero who would lead a literal army in a triumphant battle against the Roman oppressors. In the second half of his Gospel, Mark describes the nature of Jesus' messiahship. In this section (Mark 8:31–10:45), the disciples discover that he is the Son of Man who came to die for others.

8:31 To predict one's death is rare, but not unknown. To predict that one will then rise from the dead, however, is startling. No wonder the disciples had trouble taking in what Jesus was saying. The fact that this prediction is repeated in Mark's Gospel (9:9,31; 10:33–34) draws attention to its central importance in understanding who Jesus is.

Son of Man. This is the title that Jesus prefers for himself. In the first century it was a rather colorless, indeterminate title (with some messianic overtones) which could be translated as "man" or even "I." This allows Jesus through his teaching to fill it with new meaning and to convey what kind of Messiah he actually is. See the note on John 1:51 in Session 4.

rejected by the elders, chief priests and teachers of the law. These three groups made up the Sanhedrin, the ruling Jewish body. While ultimately under Roman supervision, the Sanhedrin had the power to rule in cases involving Jewish law. Jesus is predicting that he will be officially rejected by Israel (see Mark 14:55).

must be killed. The death of the Messiah at the hands of Israel's official governing body played no part in popular ideas about the Messiah. This was a startling, incomprehensible announcement. Jesus knew that his death was mandated by God. It was prophesied in the vision of the Suffering Servant of the Lord in Isaiah 53, and the suffering of the righteous man in Psalm 22.

after three days rise again. This likewise was an unprecedented teaching regarding the Messiah.

8:32 *He spoke plainly.* This is in contrast to his usual style of teaching in parables, the meaning of which was sometimes veiled or obscure. This is exactly what is going to happen.

rebuke. Peter, who moments before identified Jesus as the Messiah, is startled by this teaching. It went so much against his notion of what the Messiah should do. He felt compelled to take Jesus aside and urge him to stop this line of teaching.

8:33 In response, Jesus does the same thing: he rebukes Peter.

Get behind me, Satan! Satan's essential temptation was to persuade Jesus to avoid the way of the cross on his way to receiving the kingdom (Matt. 4:8–10). To do so, however, would require that Jesus abandon his loyalty to the Father. While Peter's objection is motivated by concern, Jesus recognizes it as another appeal for him to turn away from the Father's will. This is not a rejection of Peter's genuine concern, but a dramatic way of expressing Jesus' determination not to allow anything or anyone to dissuade him from following the path God has set for him.

the things of God / the things of men. Peter was concerned with the establishment of a powerful Jewish kingdom ruled by Jesus. Jesus was concerned with the Father's will for a universal kingdom in which all people who believed in him would be reconciled to God and one another through the sacrificial death of Jesus for their sins.

8:34–38 Jesus defines what following him means. It is not glory and magic. It involves denial, cross-bearing, and losing one's life.

8:34 *he called the crowd ... along with his disciples.* By this phrase, Mark is showing that this message is intended to be heard by *everyone* who wishes to follow Jesus. While the miracles might have made it appear that the kingdom of God simply meant fulfillment and joy, Jesus makes it clear that the way to the kingdom involves self-denial and sacrifice. These words would have special meaning for the original recipients of the Gospel, the Christians in Rome (who were, in fact, suffering for the sake of Jesus during the persecution under Emperor Nero).

come after me. Discipleship is a matter of following the ways of one's teacher.

deny himself / take up his cross / follow me. To "take up a cross" was something done only by a person sentenced to death by crucifixion. This would fill the minds of Mark's readers with memories of their comrades who had been executed in this way by Nero (under the charge that to be a Christian was an act of treason to Rome). This stark image points out the fact that to be a follower of Jesus means that loyalty to him precedes all desires and ambitions, including the natural desire for self-preservation. Like Jesus, his followers are to single-mindedly pursue God's way, even when it means suffering and death.

8:35 *save his life.* The image is of a trial in which one is called upon to renounce Jesus in order to live. This would have immediate application to the Christians in Rome, who were pressed with the decision of considering whether to affirm their loyalty to Jesus (and face the persecution of the state) or deny their association with Jesus (and be allowed to live).

will lose it. That is, the person will ultimately face the judgment of God for his or her denial of Christ.

whoever loses his life ... will save it. The person who steadfastly maintains loyalty to Jesus, even in the face of death, has the sure hope of the eternal life to come.

8:36–37 These two rhetorical questions emphasize the critical nature of the decision to remain loyal to Jesus. To gain one's physical life while forfeiting one's eternal destiny is a foolish bargain. As Jim Elliot, a martyred missionary, once wrote, "He is no fool who gives what he cannot keep to gain what he cannot lose."

8:38 *ashamed of me.* This would be revealed by failing to persist in one's Christian testimony in times of persecution.

Son of Man / Father's glory / holy angels. This is apocalyptic imagery borrowed from Daniel 7:13ff. The Jewish expectation was that God's kingdom would one day be decisively and dramatically ushered in.

8 The Transfiguration—Mark 9:2–13

THREE-PART AGENDA

ICE-BREAKER
15 Minutes

BIBLE STUDY
30 Minutes

CARING TIME
15–45 Minutes

> *LEADER: Have you started working with your group about your mission—for instance, by having them review pages M3 and M6 in the center section? If you have a new person at the meeting, remember to do an appropriate ice-breaker from the center section.*

TO BEGIN THE BIBLE STUDY TIME
(Choose 1 or 2)

1. What's the tallest mountain you've ever been on?

2. When is a time you really put your foot in your mouth?

3. If you were to plan a getaway with three friends, who would you take and where would you go?

READ SCRIPTURE & DISCUSS
(If you don't have time for all the questions in this section, conclude the Bible Study [30 min.] by answering question #8.)

The disciples have discovered that Jesus is no mere teacher. Nor is he simply a prophet. He is the Messiah—God's anointed Servant who has come to bring a new order in the world.

1. How would you describe your relationship with God right now: In the valley? On the mountaintop? Climbing? Other?

2. Why was Peter's response to what he had just seen inappropriate? What caused him to react this way?

3. What questions did Peter, James and John have as they came down the mountain? What questions would you be asking?

The Transfiguration

²After six days Jesus took Peter, James and John with him and led them up a high mountain, where they were all alone. There he was transfigured before them. ³His clothes became dazzling white, whiter than anyone in the world could bleach them. ⁴And there appeared before them Elijah and Moses, who were talking with Jesus.

⁵Peter said to Jesus, "Rabbi, it is good for us to be here. Let us put up three shelters—one for you, one for Moses and one for Elijah." ⁶(He did not know what to say, they were so frightened.)

⁷Then a cloud appeared and enveloped them, and a voice came from the cloud: "This is my Son, whom I love. Listen to him!"

⁸Suddenly, when they looked around, they no longer saw anyone with them except Jesus.

⁹As they were coming down the mountain, Jesus gave them orders not to tell anyone what they had seen until the Son of Man had risen from the dead. ¹⁰They kept the matter to themselves, discussing what "rising from the dead" meant.

¹¹And they asked him, "Why do the teachers of the law say that Elijah must come first?"

¹²Jesus replied, "To be sure, Elijah does come first, and restores all things. Why then is it written that the Son of Man must suffer much and be rejected? ¹³But I tell you, Elijah has come, and they have done to him everything they wished, just as it is written about him."

4. How did Jesus answer their question about Elijah preceding the Messiah? How does Elijah's experience fore-shadow Jesus' experience (see note on v. 13)?

5. How would this experience be a help and encouragement to Jesus as he drew nearer to his time of suffering and death?

6. How can you encourage your pastor or others in ministry in the coming week?

7. When have you experienced a powerful spiritual moment? What effect did it have on your life?

8. God told Peter, James and John, "This is my Son ... Listen to him!" (v. 7). When it comes to listening to Jesus, what have you found helpful?

CARING TIME

(Choose 1 or 2 of these questions before taking prayer requests and closing in prayer. Be sure to pray for the empty chair.)

1. What is your dream for the future mission of this group?

2. How are you doing with spending personal time in prayer and Bible Study?

3. How can this group help you in prayer?

Summary. Events begin to gather speed. The disciples have discovered that Jesus is no mere teacher (no matter how gifted and special he is), nor is he simply a prophet (no matter how powerful he might be). He is the Messiah—God's anointed Servant who has come to bring a new order in the world. The remaining sessions focus on how Jesus opens the way into the kingdom of God by his death and resurrection. Here in the Transfiguration, God affirms once again that Jesus is his beloved Son, and he declares (via the three apostles who witness these events) that Jesus is, indeed, the promised one whose coming was foretold in the Old Testament.

The account of the Transfiguration is similar to the baptism of Jesus (Mark 1:9–11) in some interesting ways. The baptism of Jesus opened the first half of the Gospel of Mark (after some preliminary words from the Old Testament and from John the Baptist). The Transfiguration opens the second half following some defining words by Jesus. In both incidents, the voice of God affirms that Jesus is his special Son. Both draw heavily on the Old Testament for their meaning. As the baptism of Jesus foreshadows his death, so the Transfiguration foreshadows his resurrection.

9:2 *After six days.* With this phrase Mark connects the Transfiguration with Jesus' prediction that "some who are standing here will not taste death before they see the kingdom of God come with power" (Mark 9:1). The mention of "six days" is probably also an allusion to Exodus 24:15–18, where the story is told of Moses going up the mountain and remaining six days until he is summoned into the presence of God. Thus the readers are alerted to the fact that another revelation of God is about to take place.

Peter, James and John. These three apostles come to form a sort of inner circle around Jesus. Mark has already pointed out that Jesus took only these three disciples with him when he raised Jairus' daughter (Mark 5:37–43). Here he selects them to accompany him up the mountain. These are three of the first four disciples Jesus chose (Mark 1:14–20).

a high mountain. This may well be Mt. Hermon, a mountain 9,000 feet high located 12 miles from Caesarea Philippi (though early tradition says it is Mt. Tabor located southwest of the Sea of Galilee). The physical location of the mountain is not as significant as its theological meaning. Mountains were the places where God revealed himself to the leaders of Israel in special ways. For example, God appeared to Moses on Mt. Sinai (Ex. 24) and to the prophet Elijah on Mt. Horeb (1 Kings 19).

transfigured. The word used here is *metamorphothe* (from which the word "metamorphosis" comes). It literally means "to change one's form."

9:3 *dazzling white.* The word "dazzling" (or radiant) was used to describe the glistening of highly polished metal or the sparkling of sunlight. Here the disciples witness Jesus as he is changed into a form just like God. In Revelation 1:9–18, the resurrected, glorified Jesus is described in similar terms. Brilliant, radiant light is often associated with appearances of God in the Old Testament (see Dan. 7:9).

9:4 *Elijah.* Elijah was a great prophet. The Jews expected that he would return just prior to the coming of the salvation they had been promised (Mal. 4:5–6). His presence on the mountain is to indicate that, indeed, he has come to bear witness to Jesus as the Messiah.

Moses. Moses was the greatest figure in Israel's history and tradition. He was the one to whom God gave the Law, which became the very heart of the nation. He was the one who brought the religion of Israel into being. And it was Moses who prophesied that God would one day send another prophet to lead his people: "The LORD your God will raise up for you a prophet like me from among your own brothers. You must listen to him" (Deut. 18:15). The early Christians took this to be a prophecy about Jesus (Acts 3:22–26; 7:35–37). The presence of both Moses and Elijah on the mountain is meant to indicate that the Old Testament Law and the Prophets, which form the core of Israel's identity, endorse Jesus as God's appointed Messiah. They witness to his greatness and superiority over them.

9:5 *shelters.* Peter might have had in mind the huts of intertwined branches that were put up at the Festival of Tabernacles to commemorate Israel's time in the wilderness. Or he might be thinking of the "tent of meeting" where God met with Moses. In making this suggestion, Peter shows his quite understandable confusion about this event. Did it mark the full arrival of the kingdom? Did this mean that Jesus had come into his glory without the suffering he told them about?

9:6 frightened. Throughout the Bible, whenever God is manifested before people, the human response is one of fear and being undone (Ex. 3:5–6; 20:18–19; Judg. 6:20–23; Isa. 6:5; Dan. 10:7–8; Rev. 1:17).

9:7 a cloud. The Old Testament often speaks of clouds as one of the phenomena which accompanies an appearance of God (Ex. 16:10; 19:9; 24:15–18; 40:34–38). Clouds are signs of his majesty and serve to veil his full glory from the eyes of mortals (who would otherwise be totally overwhelmed). This cloud is a symbol of the presence of God.

a voice. Once again, as he did at the baptism of Jesus (Mark 1:11), God declares that Jesus is his Son.

This is my Son, whom I love. By means of this incident, it is revealed that not only is Jesus the Messiah (as the disciples have just confessed), he is also the Son of God. Both titles are necessary for a full understanding of his nature and role.

Listen to him! This is a quotation from Moses' great prophecy about the coming prophet (see note for 9:4). The new prophet, whose authority and glory would supersede that of Moses, was on the scene. This is a divine testimony to his authority.

9:8 In an instant, the overwhelming experience of God's glory was gone. Moses, Elijah, and God himself had all borne witness to these three disciples regarding the person of Jesus. Mark has answered once and for all the question about Jesus' identity which had been building throughout the first eight chapters of his Gospel. Now the disciples are to learn more fully what discipleship to the Messiah, the Son of God, really involves.

9:9–11 What must have seemed so clear on the mountain became obscure as the disciples walked down. Jesus again introduces the thought of his impending death, which to the disciples seems totally out of context with what they have just experienced. They wonder if there is some other meaning to the notion of "rising from the dead." Then their thoughts run to the meaning of the Jewish expectation that Elijah will come to inaugurate the kingdom. Was that what had happened on the mountain? Their questions spring from confusion over the sig-

nificance of the Transfiguration and Jesus' teaching about the suffering and death of the Messiah.

9:9 not to tell. Once again, Jesus commands silence (see note on Mark 8:30 in Session 7). The meaning of this event cannot be understood until Jesus dies and rises again. Then it will be clear what kind of Messiah he is and what it means to be the Son of God.

the Son of Man. See notes on Mark 8:31 in Session 7 and on John 1:51 in Session 4.

9:11 Elijah must come first. Elijah, a prophet who had called Israel to be faithful to God during a time of widespread apostasy, never died but was taken up into heaven by God (2 Kings 2:1–12). The Jews believed that God would send Elijah back before the Messiah appeared to again call Israel to faithfulness. This was substantiated by the prophecy in Malachi 4:5–6.

9:12 To be sure, Elijah does come first. Here in the Transfiguration the long-expected Elijah comes. However, as verse 13 shows, Jesus asserts that Elijah has come in a second sense. John the Baptist came in the spirit and power of Elijah by being the forerunner of the Messiah.

Why then is it written. Jesus does not specify which Old Testament passage he has in mind. However, a passage like Isaiah 53:3 would explain his statement here (and in Mark 8:31) that the Son of Man "must suffer" and die. While it seems incongruous to the disciples that the Messiah must suffer, Jesus reminds them that Elijah himself suffered at the hands of King Ahab and Queen Jezebel (1 Kings 19:1–10).

9:13 Elijah has come, and they have done to him everything they wished, just as it is written about him. John the Baptist suffered and died at the hands of Herod and Herodias (see Mark 6:14–29), paralleling Elijah's experience in the past. John's suffering and death foreshadow what awaits Jesus as well. Jesus is shattering the illusion that God's anointed messengers move easily into triumph. Elijah and John are two great men of God from Israel's past and present who were rejected and persecuted by the leaders of the people. Thus, it should come as no surprise to learn that the Messiah himself will experience the same rejection.

9 The Lord's Supper—Mark 14:12–26

THREE-PART AGENDA

ICE-BREAKER
15 Minutes

BIBLE STUDY
30 Minutes

CARING TIME
15–45 Minutes

LEADER: To help you identify an Apprentice / Leader for a new small group (or if you have a new person at this meeting), see the listing of ice-breakers on page M7 of the center section. You may want to celebrate the Lord's Supper as a group in place of the usual Caring Time.

TO BEGIN THE BIBLE STUDY TIME
(Choose 1 or 2)

1. What is one of your favorite places to eat?

2. What is your favorite hymn or praise song?

3. Growing up, what occasion did your family celebrate with a big meal? Whose house was it at? Where did people sit? What was the main course?

READ SCRIPTURE & DISCUSS
(If you don't have time for all the questions in this section, conclude the Bible Study [30 min.] by answering question #7.)

1. How does your church go about observing the Lord's Supper? How often?

2. What is one of the most memorable Communion services you have ever experienced?

3. How is the Lord's Supper related to the Passover and what preparations did this meal require (see notes on v. 12)?

4. What does Jesus say about his betrayer (vv. 18–21)? How do the disciples react to this "bombshell"?

The Lord's Supper

[12]On the first day of the Feast of Unleavened Bread, when it was customary to sacrifice the Passover lamb, Jesus' disciples asked him, "Where do you want us to go and make preparations for you to eat the Passover?"

[13]So he sent two of his disciples, telling them, "Go into the city, and a man carrying a jar of water will meet you. Follow him. [14]Say to the owner of the house he enters, 'The Teacher asks: Where is my guest room, where I may eat the Passover with my disciples?' [15]He will show you a large upper room, furnished and ready. Make preparations for us there."

[16]The disciples left, went into the city and found things just as Jesus had told them. So they prepared the Passover.

[17]When evening came, Jesus arrived with the Twelve. [18]While they were reclining at the table eating, he said, "I tell you the truth, one of you will betray me—one who is eating with me."

[19]They were saddened, and one by one they said to him, "Surely not I?"

[20]"It is one of the Twelve," he replied, "one who dips bread into the bowl with me. [21]The Son of Man will go just as it is written about him. But woe to that man who betrays the Son of Man! It would be better for him if he had not been born."

[22]While they were eating, Jesus took bread, gave thanks and broke it, and gave it to his disciples, saying, "Take it; this is my body."

[23]Then he took the cup, gave thanks and offered it to them, and they all drank from it.

[24]"This is my blood of the[a] covenant, which is poured out for many," he said to them. [25]"I tell you the truth, I will not drink again of the fruit of the vine until that day when I drink it anew in the kingdom of God."

[26]When they had sung a hymn, they went out to the Mount of Olives.

[a]24 Some manuscripts *the new*

5. What profound new meaning does Jesus give to the Passover bread (v. 22) and to the Passover cup (vv. 23–24)?

6. Why is it important for Christians to observe Communion? What does the Lord's Supper mean to you?

7. Before you take Communion the next time, what can you do to make it more spiritually meaningful?

CARING TIME

(Choose 1 or 2 of these questions before taking prayer requests and closing in prayer. Be sure to pray for the empty chair.)

1. Have you started working on your group mission— to choose an Apprentice / Leader from your group to start a new group in the future? (See Mission / Multiplication on page M3.)

2. What is something for which you are particularly thankful?

3. How can the group pray for you?

Summary. The Last Supper plays an important role in Matthew, Mark and Luke. Through this meal, Jesus formally introduces the fact that his death is the means by which a new covenant would be established between God and his people. It is this meal that declares Jesus' continuing presence with his people, and gives meaning to Jesus' death as a sacrifice for sins. At Passover, a lamb was sacrificed as a means of atoning for the sins of the people. In the same way, Jesus' death is a sacrifice which leads God to "pass over" (or forgive) the sins of those who entrust themselves to him.

14:12 *On the first day of the Feast of Unleavened Bread.* The Feast of Unleavened Bread, which commemorated the deliverance of Israel from Egypt (Ex. 12:14–20), did not officially start until the day after the Passover. However, by the first century this feast was coupled with the Passover so that there was a week of feasting. The day on which the lambs were sacrificed was sometimes referred to as the first day of the Feast of Unleavened Bread.

sacrifice the Passover lamb. Passover was a feast in which the people of Israel celebrated how God "passed over" them as he brought judgment upon the Egyptians who had for so long mistreated Israel (see Ex. 12). Each pilgrim sacrificed his own lamb in the temple. A priest caught the blood in a bowl and this was thrown on the altar. After removing parts of the lamb for sacrifice, the carcass was returned to the pilgrim to be roasted and eaten for Passover. Josephus estimated that 250,000 lambs were killed at Passover. On this particular Passover, God would once again rescue his people, though in a totally unexpected way—namely through the death of the Messiah.

make preparations. The disciples would have to set out the unleavened bread and the wine, collect the bitter herbs such as horseradish and chicory (which represented the bitterness of slavery), make the sauce of dried fruit, spices, and wine in which the bread was dipped (which represented how the Israelites had to make bricks), and roast the lamb on an open fire (which reminded the people of the lambs which were sacrificed at the original Passover).

eat the Passover. The meal begins with a blessing, the passing of bread, and drinking from the first of four cups of wine. Then psalms are sung and the story of the deliverance read, followed by the second cup of wine and the eating of the bread, herbs, and the sauce (into which Judas and the others dip the bread—see v. 20). Then the meal itself, with the roast lamb and the remainder of the bread, is eaten. More prayers are said and the third cup is drunk. More psalms are sung before the final cup is drunk. After that, another psalm is sung. Two short prayers end the feast. The four cups of wine represented the four promises God gave the Israelites in Exodus 6:6–7: (1) "I will bring you out from under the yoke of the Egyptians," (2) "I will free you …" (3) "I will redeem you ..." and (4) "I will take you as my own people."

14:13–16 Instructions for Jesus' arrest had already been issued (see John 11:57). Since he knew that the officials were looking for him in places away from the crowd, he would generally sleep in Bethany, which was outside the jurisdiction of the priests. However, Jews were required to eat the Passover meal in Jerusalem itself. Hence the need for secret arrangements. The irony is that Jesus knows full well that he will be betrayed from within his own circle of disciples (see Mark 14:18–21,27–31). Jesus' instructions here parallel those he gave concerning the donkey on which he first rode into the city (see Mark 11:1–6). It seems clear that he has been to Jerusalem previously when he made these arrangements. It is also clear that he is arranging the events so that they happen in such a way as to reveal who he is.

14:13 *a man carrying a jar of water.* Such a person would have been easy to spot and follow since it was highly unusual for a man to carry a jug.

14:17 *When evening came.* The Passover meal could be eaten only after sunset. What followed was a night of eager watching in which people asked: "Will this be the night when God comes again to deliver his people from bondage?"

14:18 *reclining at the table.* People would eat festive meals by lying on couches or cushions arranged around a low table.

I tell you the truth. Literally, this is "Amen," a word used to announce a solemn declaration.

one of you / one who is eating with me. These words "set the pronouncement in the context of Psalm 41:9, where the poor but righteous sufferer laments that his intimate friend whom he has trusted and who ate his bread had 'lifted up his heel' against him" (Lane).

14:20 *one who dips bread into the bowl with me.* This was the bowl of sauce. To eat together was a sign of friendship.

14:21 *The Son of Man.* See notes on Mark 8:31 in Session 7 and on John 1:51 in Session 4.

will go just as it is written about him. Passages such as Isaiah 53:1–6 point to the suffering of God's chosen servant.

It would be better for him if he had not been born. This is a stern warning of the judgment to come upon Judas (and others) who turn their backs on Jesus.

14:22–26 Jesus' celebration of the Last Supper provides the model for the way the church came to celebrate Communion (see 1 Cor. 11:23–26). His use of the bread and the cup in a symbolic way (as a means of teaching) was consistent with the way in which the various elements of the Passover meal were used symbolically (e.g., the bowl of salt water was used to remind them of the tears shed in Egypt and of the Red Sea through which they passed). The symbols in the Passover meal pointed back to the first covenant God made with Israel, while Jesus' words here at the Last Supper pointed forward to his death and the new covenant which would result from it.

14:22 *took bread, gave thanks and broke it, and gave it to his disciples.* Commonly at Passover, bread was broken and distributed prior to the meal as a reminder of how God had provided bread for his people in the wilderness. Jesus' action at this point in the meal would be unusual, calling attention to its new, special meaning.

this is my body. Jesus adds a radically new interpretation to the bread. From now on, they are to see it as representing his body. As they share in the bread, they share in his life, mission and destiny.

14:23 *cup.* Lane argues that this was the third cup passed around at the end of the meal, which stood for the promise of redemption. Jesus relates the Passover cup of red wine to the renewal of the covenant of God with his people through his sacrificial death. It is in this way that redemption will truly come.

gave thanks. The Greek word "to give thanks" is *eucharisto*, from which the English word Eucharist is derived.

14:24 *covenant.* In general terms, a covenant is a treaty between two parties. Such an agreement was often sealed by the sacrifice of an animal. In specific terms it refers to the arrangement that God made with Israel (see Ex. 24:1–8) which was dependent on Israel's obedience. Now (as anticipated in Jer. 31:31–33) a new covenant is established which is made dependent on Jesus' obedience (his sacrificial death). A covenant of law becomes a covenant of love.

blood ... poured out. The pouring out of blood was a symbol of a violent death (see Gen. 4:10–11; Deut. 19:10; Matt. 23:35). This phrase points to the type of death Jesus would experience.

14:25 *I will not drink again of the fruit of the vine.* Apparently, Jesus does not drink the fourth and final cup, which symbolizes how God has gathered his people to himself. Instead, he will wait until the messianic banquet at the close of the age to celebrate the fulfillment of that promise.

the kingdom of God. The presence of God's reign was often pictured as a great banquet.

14:26 The Hallel (Psalms 113–118) was sung at the Passover; the first part (Psalms 113–114) prior to the meal, and the second part, mentioned here, after the meal (Psalms 115–118). The rich promises of Psalm 118 would be on Jesus' lips as he leaves the room to face the Crucifixion only a few hours away.

10 Gethsemane—Mark 14:32–42

THREE-PART AGENDA

ICE-BREAKER	BIBLE STUDY	CARING TIME
15 Minutes	30 Minutes	15–45 Minutes

>  **LEADER:** To help you identify an Apprentice / Leader for a new small group (or if you have a new person at this meeting), see the listing of ice-breakers on page M7 of the center section.

TO BEGIN THE BIBLE STUDY TIME
(Choose 1 or 2)

1. When do you have trouble staying awake: Watching the late news? In church? Driving at night? Other?

2. What do you do to stay awake when you have to? Who needs the most sleep in your family?

3. Where do you like to pray?

READ SCRIPTURE & DISCUSS
(If you don't have time for all the questions in this section, conclude the Bible Study [30 min.] by answering question #7.)

1. What three friends would you call in a crisis?

2. Why did Jesus bring along Peter, James and John? What did Jesus ask of the disciples?

3. What did Jesus ask God when he prayed? What do you learn about Jesus from this passage?

4. Jesus told Peter, "Watch and pray" because "the spirit is willing, but the body is weak" (v. 38). How do these words apply to you?

Gethsemane

32They went to a place called Gethsemane, and Jesus said to his disciples, "Sit here while I pray." 33He took Peter, James and John along with him, and he began to be deeply distressed and troubled. 34"My soul is overwhelmed with sorrow to the point of death," he said to them. "Stay here and keep watch."

35Going a little farther, he fell to the ground and prayed that if possible the hour might pass from him. 36"Abba,a Father," he said, "everything is possible for you. Take this cup from me. Yet not what I will, but what you will."

37Then he returned to his disciples and found them sleeping. "Simon," he said to Peter, "are you asleep? Could you not keep watch for one hour? 38Watch and pray so that you will not fall into temptation. The spirit is willing, but the body is weak."

39Once more he went away and prayed the same thing. 40When he came back, he again found them sleeping, because their eyes were heavy. They did not know what to say to him.

41Returning the third time, he said to them, "Are you still sleeping and resting? Enough! The hour has come. Look, the Son of Man is betrayed into the hands of sinners. 42Rise! Let us go! Here comes my betrayer!"

a36 Aramaic for *Father*

5. When was a time you were deeply distressed and troubled? What did you do?

6. What have you found helpful in determining God's will for your life?

7. What is the biggest issue you are facing in your life right now?

CARING TIME

(Choose 1 or 2 of these questions before taking prayer requests and closing in prayer. Be sure to pray for the empty chair.)

1. Where in your life do you need to submit to God and do his will?

2. Rate this past week on a scale of 1 (terrible) to 10 (great). What's the outlook for this week?

3. How would you like this group to pray for you?

Notes—Mark 14:32–42

Summary. This scene follows immediately after the Lord's Supper. Two themes dominate this story: Jesus' continued obedience to God (despite his dread of what was coming) and the disciples' continued failure to grasp what lay ahead for Jesus.

14:32 *Gethsemane.* This was an olive orchard in an estate at the foot of the Mount of Olives just outside the eastern wall of Jerusalem. The name literally means "an oil press" (for making olive oil).

14:33 *Peter, James and John.* As in the past, these three men (who form the inner circle around Jesus) accompany Jesus during a time of great significance (see Mark 9:2–8). Interestingly, neither the rebuke of Peter (Mark 8:32), nor the self-centered request of James and John (Mark 10:35–40), nor the warning of Peter's upcoming denial (Mark 14:27–31) has damaged their relationship with Jesus. Observing that each of these men has vowed to stay with Jesus through thick or thin (see Mark 10:38–39; 14:29,31), Lane comments: "The failure to understand what it means to share Jesus' destiny and to be identified with his sufferings, rather than privileged status, appears to be the occasion for the isolation of the three from the others. Their glib self-confidence exposes them to grave peril of failure in the struggle they confront, and for that reason they are commanded to be vigilant." What Jesus asks them to share with him is not glory (which they wanted) but sorrow (which they kept denying would come, e.g., Mark 8:31–32).

deeply distressed. Literally, this is filled with "shuddering awe." Jesus is filled with a deep, deep sorrow as the full impact of what his submission to God will mean overwhelms him.

14:34 *keep watch.* This was an invitation for the disciples to join him in preparation for the severe trial that was soon to come. While it expresses Jesus' desire for human companionship in his time of crisis, it also points out that these men need to prepare themselves as well. Verses 37–41 show that his concern was for how they would face the fact of his arrest and death.

14:35 *a little farther.* A few yards more.

fell to the ground. This accents the emotional distress he was feeling. He is physically overwhelmed by the depth of sorrow and anxiety he feels.

prayed. It was customary at the time for people to pray aloud. Therefore, the disciples heard (and remembered) his prayer. This is the third time in Mark that Jesus has been shown in prayer (see also Mark 1:35; 6:46).

the hour. This word is often used to refer to an event that represents a crucial turning point in God's plan for a person or for the world (see v. 41; also Mark 13:32). In reference to Jesus, it specifically refers to his crucifixion (see also John 12:23ff). Jesus' plea is that there might be some way for God's plan to be fulfilled without him having to face this particular "hour."

14:36 *Abba.* This is Aramaic for "Father." This is how a child would address their father, i.e., "Daddy." This was not a title that was used in prayer in the first century.

this cup. Like the word "hour," "cup" was also used as an image referring to the destiny God had in store for a person. In some cases it refers to "the cup of salvation" the Lord gives his people to drink (Ps. 16:5; 116:13). Quite often the "cup of the Lord" was used in reference to divine judgment (Ps. 75:8; Isa. 51:17; Jer. 25:15; Ezek. 23:32–33; Rev. 16:19). To experience God's judgment is like being forced to drink large gulps of strong, bitter wine; it leaves a person sick, staggering and totally unable to function. By this image, Jesus acknowledges that his impending death is not simply a human tragedy, but an act of divine judgment (see also Mark 10:38–39). It is this aspect of what he faces that so frightens him. He must drink of the cup of God's wrath against sin.

Yet not what I will, but what you will. This is the classic expression of Jesus' submission to God. While his personal desire was to avoid the cross, his deeper commitment was to do the Father's will even though it included the cross. Today many people tend to use this phrase when they are unsure of what God's will is in their personal situation (i.e., "I pray you will heal my uncle, Lord; but your will, not mine, be done"). This is not the case here. Jesus had no doubt as to what the Father's will was. God's will was horribly clear to him and he recoiled from it. For Jesus, this phrase is an expression of his final resolve. Although the prospect of the cross seemed crushing to him, this statement expresses his commitment to pursue God's will despite the cost.

14:37 *sleeping.* It was late (the Passover could extend up to midnight) and they had drunk at least four cups of wine in connection with the Passover meal (see notes on Mark 14:12 in Session 9).

Simon ... are you asleep? Jesus had earlier warned Peter that he would soon disavow ever having known Jesus, a charge Peter denied emphatically (Mark 14:29–31). Despite this warning, even Peter fails to prepare himself to face what was to come.

one hour. This time the word is used literally (see note on v. 35). Despite Jesus' clear warning that a major crisis was coming, Peter and the other two disciples could not even take a relatively short amount of time to prepare themselves.

14:38 *Watch and pray.* To "watch" means to "be spiritually alert," lest they fall into the "temptation" to be unfaithful to God. This call to watch and pray echoes what is found in the parable about the owner of the house (Mark 13:35–37) referring to the time of the coming of the Son of Man in power and glory (Mark 13:26–27). It may be that Mark intends his readers to learn a lesson from the three disciples here. Their subsequent denial and desertion of Jesus indicates what happens to those who fail to prepare themselves spiritually. The owner of the house returns and the servants are not carrying out their tasks. In contrast, those who follow Jesus are to be spiritually awake at all times so they are not caught off guard when the times of trial and crisis arrive. This would have special relevance for the church in Rome to which Mark was writing as they faced persecution under Nero. Will they maintain vigilance and faith, or will they "fall asleep" and cave in under the pressure to deny they are disciples of Christ?

temptation. The trial or test that is about to come upon them is not merely something that might cause physical pain. It is one that could lead them to deny their loyalty to God himself.

The spirit is willing, but the body is weak. This is not saying that the disciples' hearts are in the right place, but they are just too tired to do what Jesus says! It is better to translate "body" as "flesh" in that it refers not simply to a person's body but one's human nature. It is an observation that although God's Spirit is available to help them, the orientation of their lives is still not toward God (see Ps. 51:12). To the very end, even the three disciples most intimately connected with Jesus fail to understand his teaching about what it means to be the Messiah. Had they done so, they would have prepared themselves for the danger that lay ahead. They would also have helped Jesus as he prepared for the impending crisis. As it is, Jesus is all alone in his sorrow.

14:39–40 A second time Jesus goes off to pray, but returns to find the disciples asleep.

They did not know what to say to him. This is reflective of the householder's servants who are left without excuse when confronted with the fact that they have failed to carry out their duties faithfully (Mark 13:36). The disciples simply cannot grasp the pressing importance of the situation they face. Jesus is overwhelmed with the gravity of the moment, and faces his own struggle with whether or not to follow the Father's will. But they are not sufficiently gripped by what is happening to be emotionally stirred to prayer.

14:41 *the third time.* Jesus had earlier warned Peter that he would deny him three times (Mark 14:30). Now Jesus comes to Peter three times to urge him to pray and become prepared for what is to come. However, as in the other two times, Peter and the others are asleep again.

Are you still sleeping and resting? This is an ironic note of rebuke. Right up to the moment of crisis, the disciples fail to recognize what is happening. They have not prepared themselves at all.

The hour has come. See note on verse 35.

into the hands of sinners. This refers to the religious authorities that Jesus confronted throughout Mark 11:1–13:37 who have corrupted the offices they hold. The irony of this assessment is that the term "sinners" was used by these religious leaders to refer to those Jews who did not live by the Law and to all Gentiles. In fact, it is a term they have earned by their actions.

14:42 *Rise! Let us go!* Having resolved to do the Father's will, Jesus takes the initiative to approach the crowd coming to arrest him. This action illustrates the words of John's Gospel when Jesus declared, "No one takes (my life) from me, but I lay it down of my own accord" (John 10:18).

THREE-PART AGENDA

ICE-BREAKER
15 Minutes

BIBLE STUDY
30 Minutes

CARING TIME
15–45 Minutes

> *LEADER: To help you identify people who might form the core of a new small group (or if a new person comes to this meeting), see the listing of ice-breakers on page M7 of the center section.*

TO BEGIN THE BIBLE STUDY TIME
(Choose 1 or 2)

1. Growing up, who were the bullies in your life? How did they pick on you?

2. When have you been in a *wild* crowd: At a concert? Sporting event? Protest march? Church? Other?

3. How do you go about making a difficult decision?

READ SCRIPTURE & DISCUSS
(If you don't have time for all the questions in this section, conclude the Bible Study [30 min.] by answering question #7.)

1. When have you been accused of something you didn't do?

2. Why did the Jewish leaders bring Jesus before Pilate? Why was Jesus so silent throughout his trial?

3. What is Pilate's overriding concern in this trial? How would you describe Pilate?

4. In this passage, how do you think Jesus was viewed by these people: The Sanhedrin? Pilate? The crowd? Barabbas? The soldiers?

Jesus Before Pilate

15 *Very early in the morning, the chief priests, with the elders, the teachers of the law and the whole Sanhedrin, reached a decision. They bound Jesus, led him away and handed him over to Pilate.*

²"Are you the king of the Jews?" asked Pilate.

"Yes, it is as you say," Jesus replied.

³The chief priests accused him of many things. ⁴So again Pilate asked him, "Aren't you going to answer? See how many things they are accusing you of."

⁵But Jesus still made no reply, and Pilate was amazed.

⁶Now it was the custom at the Feast to release a prisoner whom the people requested. ⁷A man called Barabbas was in prison with the insurrectionists who had committed murder in the uprising. ⁸The crowd came up and asked Pilate to do for them what he usually did.

⁹"Do you want me to release to you the king of the Jews?" asked Pilate, ¹⁰knowing it was out of envy that the chief priests had handed Jesus over to him. ¹¹But the chief priests stirred up the crowd to have Pilate release Barabbas instead.

¹²"What shall I do, then, with the one you call the king of the Jews?" Pilate asked them.

¹³"Crucify him!" they shouted.

¹⁴"Why? What crime has he committed?" asked Pilate.

But they shouted all the louder, "Crucify him!"

¹⁵Wanting to satisfy the crowd, Pilate released Barabbas to them. He had Jesus flogged, and handed him over to be crucified.

The Soldiers Mock Jesus

¹⁶The soldiers led Jesus away into the palace (that is, the Praetorium) and called together the whole company of soldiers. ¹⁷They put a purple robe on him, then twisted together a crown of thorns and set it on him. ¹⁸And they began to call out to him, "Hail, king of the Jews!" ¹⁹Again and again they struck him on the head with a staff and spit on him. Falling on their knees, they paid homage to him. ²⁰And when they had mocked him, they took off the purple robe and put his own clothes on him. Then they led him out to crucify him.

5. How do you feel when you read verses 16–20?

6. When have you gone along with something even though it didn't feel right?

7. How does the story of Barabbas illustrate what Jesus did for you?

8. What can you do to stand by Jesus even when it's unpopular?

CARING TIME

(Choose 1 or 2 of these questions before taking prayer requests and closing in prayer. Be sure to pray for the empty chair.)

1. Who would you choose as the leader if this group "gave birth" to a new small group? Who else would you choose to be part of the leadership core for a new group?

2. How has God been at work in your life this past week?

3. How can the group pray for you this week?

51

Summary. In Mark 14:53–65, Jesus was brought before the Sanhedrin (the Jewish high court consisting of 71 men). He was found guilty of blasphemy (defaming the character of God), a crime meriting death in the Jewish system. However, the Sanhedrin's authority was limited by the Roman government, and the Jewish leaders did not have the right to carry out capital punishment. Only Rome could do that. Therefore, the leaders brought him to Pilate, the Roman governor of the area, in hopes that he would likewise find Jesus guilty of a crime meriting death. While the trial before the Sanhedrin was conducted secretly, out of the eye of the public, the trial before Pilate was held openly in a public forum.

15:1 *Very early.* The Roman court began at daybreak. This made it necessary for the Sanhedrin to meet in an all-night session to prepare their case against Jesus. They were anxious to get a quick conviction before those loyal to Jesus could find out what was going on.

decision. While the Sanhedrin could sentence a person to death, it had no authority to actually carry out that order (see John 18:31; the incident with Stephen in Acts 7:57 appears to have been more a case of mob action than judicial process). Because of this and because of their fear of the people who supported Jesus, they needed to appeal to the Roman governor to give his approval to their decision. A Roman court would consider blasphemy merely a matter of Jewish religious scruples, not a crime requiring capital punishment. Consequently, the Sanhedrin needed to work out how to present the case to Pilate so as to ensure Jesus' death. Their decision was that when they brought Jesus to Pilate they would charge him with treason against Caesar (see Luke 23:2).

led him away. They probably took him to the palace of Herod the Great. It was here where Pilate would stay when he came to Jerusalem from his official residence in Caesarea. Pilate was probably in Jerusalem to enforce Roman authority during the great gathering of pilgrims in Jerusalem for Passover. During such feasts, the Roman presence was made very visible in order to discourage any attempts at insurrection.

Pilate. Pontius Pilate was the fifth procurator of Judea. He served from A.D. 26–36. Historians of the time called him an "inflexible, merciless and obstinate" man who disliked the Jews and their customs.

15:2–5 Mark briefly describes Jesus' interrogation by Pilate. The Roman trial consisted of the accusation followed by an examination of the defendant by the magistrate. Once a ruling had been made, it was carried out immediately.

15:2 Pilate would have been given a written deposition stating the charges against Jesus. Having read the charges, he now addresses the accused.

king of the Jews. This is how the Sanhedrin translated the Jewish title "Messiah" to Pilate. While in a sense this was an accurate rendering of the Hebrew term into Greek, this translation of the title certainly made it appear that Jesus was asserting that he, not Caesar, was the king to whom the Jews owed loyalty (see John 19:12). This would clearly be a capital offense. At this point, Pilate probably viewed Jesus as the leader of a resistance movement. There is great irony in this title. Jesus has consistently refused to be the military Messiah imagined by Jewish popular culture, and yet now he will be condemned as a guerrilla! Likewise, Pilate's question was probably laced with sarcasm. It might be paraphrased, "So ... do you, having been beaten and rejected by your own people, still fancy yourself to be their king?" This title is used six times in this chapter. While the religious authorities have manipulated the meaning of this title to work against Jesus, it remains a true statement of who he is.

Yes, it is as you say. This is an enigmatic expression. Literally, it reads "You say so" (New Revised Standard Version). By this statement Jesus accepts the title, but puts Pilate in the position to take responsibility for what he has said.

15:3 *accused him of many things.* Luke 23:2,5 gives a sense of the kinds of charges the authorities made against Jesus. They accused him of opposing the payment of taxes to Rome, of stirring up people from Galilee and Judea to insurrection, and of claiming to be the rightful king of the Jews. All of these things would be seen as a direct affront against Rome.

15:4–5 All the Gospels mention how Jesus remained silent before Pilate in the face of his charges. Seeing how his teachings had been so badly twisted in order to be used against him, there was no point in speaking. The ears of his accusers were sealed against him. Isaiah 53:7–8 speaks of how God's servant will be silent before those who accuse him falsely. If the leaders refuse to see that his whole life is a witness against the charges being made against him, words will make no difference at this point. This scene would also be of special import to the original recipients of the Gospel, some of whom would face a situation very similar to that which Jesus faced. Here, they see how he dealt with false accusations with dignity and trust in the purposes of God.

15:6–15 Pilate realized that the Sanhedrin was not motivated by any loyalty to Rome. He also recognized that Jesus was no threat to the state and that the Sanhedrin was merely using him as a pawn to get Jesus executed. However, as John 19:12 points out, Pilate could not simply release Jesus. The Sanhedrin had made it clear that should he do so they would spread the news to Rome that Pilate had dismissed the case of a man who claimed to be a rival king to Caesar. In an attempt to avoid this dilemma, Pilate appealed to a custom of granting amnesty to a prisoner who the masses called upon him to free. It may have been a local custom during Pilate's governorship as an attempt to win favor with the Jews. As Pilate saw a crowd gathering to make their appeal for amnesty, his plan was to get them to demand the release of Jesus. Thus, he could claim to have released Jesus because of the will of the people.

15:7 *Barabbas.* Nothing is known of Barabbas, but probably he was a prominent member of a failed revolt against Rome. Guerrilla attacks against Roman authority were not uncommon in Judea, where people deeply resented Roman rule. The irony here is that this name means "son of the father." While rejecting the true Son of the Father, the authorities chose to free the very type of man they falsely accuse Jesus of being.

15:8 *the crowd.* Popular representations of this scene often picture this as a crowd of people composed of many of the very same pilgrims who hailed Jesus as the one "who comes in the name of the Lord" (Mark 11:9) when he entered Jerusalem a week earlier. It is as though the crowd had somehow turned against him. In fact, it is most likely that this crowd did not assemble because of Jesus at all, but came to Pilate precisely to request the release

of Barabbas. It must be remembered that Jesus was arrested secretly at night, tried by the Sanhedrin in a closed-door session, and brought to Pilate at dawn the next morning. His closest followers had fled. Hence, there was little time or opportunity for anyone to hear of his arrest and to gather at the palace for his trial.

15:9 *the king of the Jews.* This is a deliberate jibe at the Jewish authorities. Pilate is willing to release the one claiming to be their king, for he sees no threat at all in Jesus. In this way, Pilate, in effect, minimizes the significance of the Jews as a threat to Rome.

15:11 The crowd, having come for the sake of Barabbas, was not to be dissuaded by Pilate. The religious authorities likewise encouraged them to demand Barabbas' release and not Jesus'.

15:14 *Why? What crime has he committed?* By this Mark underscores the point that Jesus was innocent of all charges brought against him. Like the Suffering Servant of the Lord in Isaiah 53:9, Jesus "had done no violence, nor was any deceit in his mouth."

15:15 *released Barabbas.* The death of Jesus (who is innocent) in the place of Barabbas (who is guilty) portrays the atoning sacrifice of Christ in the simplest of terms: man to man. It explains what Jesus meant in Mark 10:45 when he said that he came to "give his life as a ransom for many."

flogged. This was a terrible punishment. Soldiers would use a leather thong, into which pieces of bone and lead had been woven, to lash a naked and bound prisoner. The flesh would be cut to shreds.

15:16–20 The Roman soldiers mock Jesus as the Sanhedrin had done before them (see Mark 14:65). Whereas the Sanhedrin mocked the idea that he was the Messiah, the soldiers mock the idea that he is king. This whole scene is full of the humiliation of God's Messiah being ridiculed and abused by the oppressors of God's people.

15:16 *soldiers.* Probably the troops that had accompanied Pilate on his trip from Caesarea.

15:17 *a purple robe.* This was a symbol of royalty.

12 The Crucifixion—Mark 15:22–41

THREE-PART AGENDA

ICE-BREAKER
15 Minutes

BIBLE STUDY
30 Minutes

CARING TIME
15–45 Minutes

> *LEADER: Has your group discussed its plans on what to study after this course is finished? What about the mission project described on page M6 in the center section?*

TO BEGIN THE BIBLE STUDY TIME
(Choose 1 or 2)

1. Do you wear or carry a cross? Why or why not?

2. What insults really bothered you when you were a kid?

3. When have you felt most alone?

READ SCRIPTURE & DISCUSS
(If you don't have time for all the questions in this section, conclude the Bible Study [30 min.] by answering question #7.)

1. Whose death (other than Christ's) has affected you most?

2. What irony do you see in: The sign posted on the cross (v. 26)? Jesus being ridiculed for his ability to save others but not himself (vv. 29–32)?

3. What was the significance of the temple curtain being torn in two (see note on v. 38)?

4. On a scale of 1 (wide open) to 10 (closed tight), how would you describe the "curtain" between you and God right now?

5. How do you feel when you think about what Jesus did for you?

Rd. pts of Ps. 22 1-8, 17-18

54

The Crucifixion

²²They brought Jesus to the place called Golgotha (which means The Place of the Skull). ²³Then they offered him wine mixed with myrrh, but he did not take it. ²⁴And they crucified him. Dividing up his clothes, they cast lots to see what each would get.

²⁵It was the third hour when they crucified him. ²⁶The written notice of the charge against him read: THE KING OF THE JEWS. ²⁷ They crucified two robbers with him, one on his right and one on his left. ²⁹Those who passed by hurled insults at him, shaking their heads and saying, "So! You who are going to destroy the temple and build it in three days, ³⁰come down from the cross and save yourself!"

³¹In the same way the chief priests and the teachers of the law mocked him among themselves. "He saved others," they said, "but he can't save himself! ³²Let this Christ, this King of Israel, come down now from the cross, that we may see and believe." Those crucified with him also heaped insults on him.

The Death of Jesus

³³At the sixth hour darkness came over the whole land until the ninth hour. ³⁴And at the ninth hour Jesus cried out in a loud voice, "Eloi, Eloi, lama sabachthani?"—which means, "My God, my God, why have you forsaken me?"

³⁵When some of those standing near heard this, they said, "Listen, he's calling Elijah."

³⁶One man ran, filled a sponge with wine vinegar, put it on a stick, and offered it to Jesus to drink. "Now leave him alone. Let's see if Elijah comes to take him down," he said.

³⁷With a loud cry, Jesus breathed his last.

³⁸The curtain of the temple was torn in two from top to bottom. ³⁹And when the centurion, who stood there in front of Jesus, heard his cry and saw how he died, he said, "Surely this man was the Son of God!"

⁴⁰Some women were watching from a distance. Among them were Mary Magdalene, Mary the mother of James the younger and of Joses, and Salome. ⁴¹In Galilee these women had followed him and cared for his needs. Many other women who had come up with him to Jerusalem were also there.

6. What do you learn about the nature and character of Jesus in this passage?

7. How would you explain to someone what Jesus' death was all about?

8. What difference has Jesus' death made in the way you live your life?

CARING TIME

(Answer all the questions below, then take prayer requests and close with prayer.)

1. Next week will be the last session in this study. How would you like to celebrate: A dinner? A party?

2. What is the next step for this group: Start a new group? Continue with another study?

3. How can the group pray for you this week?

(If the group plans to continue, see the back inside cover for what's available from Serendipity.)

Summary. After the trial by Pilate, Jesus was beaten by the soldiers (Mark 15:16–20) before being taken out to be crucified. In this passage, the prophecies of his death at the hands of the authorities are fulfilled (Mark 8:31; 9:12,31; 10:33–34). Here, the Son of Man truly gives his life as a ransom for many (Mark 10:45), fulfilling God's plan (Mark 14:36). It is the death of Jesus that will unlock all the mysteries about how his mission will be accomplished and will open the way into the kingdom of God. While the death of Jesus has been the event that Mark has looked toward throughout his Gospel, when it actually happens he records it in a simple, stark way. The story of the death of Jesus is rich with allusions to Psalms 22 and 69 and Isaiah 53. These allusions and images indicate that the description in Mark is more than an actual account of the Crucifixion itself. It is a pictorial interpretation of the significance of Jesus' death as understood through the Old Testament prophecies.

15:22 *Golgotha.* The Aramaic word for "a skull." This was probably a small, round, bare hill outside Jerusalem.

15:23 *wine mixed with myrrh.* It was a Jewish custom to offer this pain-deadening narcotic to prisoners about to be crucified (see Ps. 69:21).

15:24 *they crucified him.* Josephus, the Jewish historian, calls crucifixion "the most wretched of all ways of dying." The person to be crucified was first stripped; his hands tied or nailed to the cross-beam, which was then lifted to the upright stake already in place; and then the feet were nailed in place. Typically death was a slow, agonizing process which occurred through shock, suffocation, and loss of blood.

Dividing up his clothes. The clothes of the condemned person belonged to the four soldiers who carried out the crucifixion (see John 19:23–24; Ps. 22:18).

15:25 *the third hour.* This would have been about 9 a.m.

15:26 *the written notice.* The crime for which the person was being crucified was specified on a whitened board fastened above the criminal.

THE KING OF THE JEWS. By posting this sign on the cross, Pilate was simply attempting to humiliate the Jews further. The intent was to communicate that Jesus' fate would be shared by anyone else who tried to assert his authority against Rome.

15:27 *robbers.* This was a term sometimes used for Zealots, the band of fiery nationalists who were committed to the violent overthrow of Rome. While "robbery" *per se* was not a capital crime, insurrection was. Perhaps these men were involved along with Barabbas in the incident mentioned in Mark 15:7. The reference to being crucified alongside criminals is probably an allusion to Isaiah 53:12.

one on his right and one on his left. Earlier on, James and John had asked to sit at Jesus' right and left hand when he came into his kingdom (Mark 10:37), a request Jesus denied. That position was left for these two criminals who shared in Jesus' death, the true means by which he would enter into his glory.

15:29–32 Clearly Psalm 22:6–8 is in Mark's mind here.

15:29 *You who are going to destroy the temple and build it in three days.* This claim is not made by Jesus in Mark's Gospel, but it is found in John 2:19, where it is treated as a prophecy of his death and resurrection.

15:31 *He saved others ... but he can't save himself.* Mark captures the irony of the profound truth coming from the lips of those who do not understand what they are saying (see also Mark 14:61–62; 15:2). It is precisely because Jesus is saving others that his own life is forfeited (Mark 10:45).

15:32 The mockers fail to reflect upon the fact that they have already seen many demonstrations of Jesus' authority, and yet still refused to believe him. Their gloating attitude matches that of the mockers described in Psalm 22:15–16.

Those crucified with him also heaped insults on him. Luke recounts how one of these men stopped his abuse and professed faith in Jesus as the Messiah (Luke 23:40–43). Mark's interest is in showing the depth of the rejection and abuse Jesus encountered right up to his death.

> *This declaration that the curtain was torn in two is Mark's way of affirming that Jesus' death has opened the way for all people to have direct access to God.*

15:33 *At the sixth hour.* This is noon.

darkness. It is disputed whether this is to be understood literally or whether it is meant as symbolic language, indicating the great significance of what was happening in terms of God's judgment. The allusion here is to Amos 8:9, where the same imagery was used to describe the "dark day" when Israel would be destroyed by the Assyrians. While there were no unusual cosmic phenomena on that day when the Assyrians invaded, for Israel it was as frightening and as destructive as if darkness had descended upon them in the middle of the day. The death of Jesus was likewise a day of judgment with profound effects for all people.

the ninth hour. This is 3 p.m.

15:34 This cry is a quote from Psalm 22:1. By echoing this cry, Jesus is identified both with the suffering of the psalmist (as he experiences unjust persecution from evil people) and with the triumph of the sufferer (as he ultimately experiences God's deliverance; see Ps. 22:19–31).

15:35 *Elijah.* The people misunderstood what Jesus said. They thought he was calling upon the ancient prophet, Elijah. This is another ironic note, since Elijah had already come in the person of John the Baptist (see note on Mark 9:11 in Session 8).

15:36 *Let's see if Elijah comes to take him down.* According to 2 Kings 2, Elijah never died; he was taken up into heaven by angels. The expectation was that Elijah would one day reappear to proclaim the advent of God's Messiah. Some in the crowd may have expected they were about to witness an eleventh hour vindication of Jesus.

15:37 *a loud cry.* This is unusual. Generally the victim of crucifixion is exhausted and unconscious at the point of death. It is almost as if Jesus voluntarily gives up his life. Perhaps what Mark mentions here is the last word in the phrase, "It is finished" (see John 19:30). This echoes the enigmatic ending of Psalm 22, which asserts that as future generations tell their children about the Lord, they will declare that "he has done it." Jesus' work of securing salvation for humanity is accomplished.

15:38 *curtain of the temple.* This curtain separated the Most Holy Place (where only the high priest could enter once a year on the Day of Atonement) from the rest of the temple. It represented the barrier which stood between the people and God. This declaration that the curtain was torn in two is Mark's way of affirming that Jesus' death has opened the way for all people to have direct access to God. The barrier has been removed because the price for sin has been fully paid. People can truly be reconciled to God. The author of Hebrews develops this imagery more fully in Hebrews 9–10.

15:39 *the Son of God.* This confession concludes the second half of Mark's Gospel. In 1:1, Mark stated that what he was writing was the Good News about Jesus the Messiah, the Son of God. The first half of the Gospel ended with the confession of Peter (a Jew) that Jesus is the Messiah (Mark 8:29); the second half ends with the confession of the centurion (a Gentile) that Jesus is the Son of God. In this context, this confession is an affirmation of the deity of Jesus.

centurion. He was the supervising officer of the soldiers who carried out the execution.

15:40 *some women.* Mark names three witnesses of the Crucifixion. Mary Magdalene was from the fishing village of Magdala on the west coast of Galilee (see Luke 8:2). The other Mary had well-known sons in the early church. Salome was the wife of Zebedee and the mother of James and John (Matt. 27:56). In contrast, all the disciples had fled.

15:41 *these women had followed him.* Luke 8:2–3 also states that there were many women who were among the first followers of Jesus. They provided the financial support which allowed him to minister.

13 The Resurrection—Matt. 28:1–20

THREE-PART AGENDA

ICE-BREAKER
15 Minutes

BIBLE STUDY
30 Minutes

CARING TIME
15–45 Minutes

> **LEADER:** Check page M7 of the center section for a good ice-breaker for this last session.

TO BEGIN THE BIBLE STUDY TIME
(Choose 1 or 2)

1. What was the high point of your week—something that brought you joy?

2. What is your favorite Easter tradition?

3. If you could go to any country as a missionary, where would you go?

READ SCRIPTURE & DISCUSS
(If you don't have time for all the questions in this section, conclude the Bible Study [30 min.] by answering question #7.)

The story of Jesus ends not with his death but with his resurrection. His death brought forgiveness for the sins of the world. His resurrection brought new life to humanity.

1. How has this group, or someone in this group, been an encouragement to you over the course of this study?

2. How do the following people react to the news of the Resurrection: The women? The guards? The chief priests? The disciples?

3. What is the central command Jesus gives his disciples? How are they to carry this out?

The Resurrection

28 *After the Sabbath, at dawn on the first day of the week, Mary Magdalene and the other Mary went to look at the tomb.*

²There was a violent earthquake, for an angel of the Lord came down from heaven and, going to the tomb, rolled back the stone and sat on it. ³His appearance was like lightning, and his clothes were white as snow. ⁴The guards were so afraid of him that they shook and became like dead men.

⁵The angel said to the women, "Do not be afraid, for I know that you are looking for Jesus, who was crucified. ⁶He is not here; he has risen, just as he said. Come and see the place where he lay. ⁷Then go quickly and tell his disciples: 'He has risen from the dead and is going ahead of you into Galilee. There you will see him.' Now I have told you."

⁸So the women hurried away from the tomb, afraid yet filled with joy, and ran to tell his disciples. ⁹Suddenly Jesus met them. "Greetings," he said. They came to him, clasped his feet and worshiped him. ¹⁰Then Jesus said to them, "Do not be afraid. Go and tell my brothers to go to Galilee; there they will see me."

¹¹While the women were on their way, some of the guards went into the city and reported to the chief priests everything that had happened. ¹²When the chief priests had met with the elders and devised a plan, they gave the soldiers a large sum of money, ¹³telling them, "You are to say, 'His disciples came during the night and stole him away while we were asleep.' ¹⁴If this report gets to the governor, we will satisfy him and keep you out of trouble." ¹⁵So the soldiers took the money and did as they were instructed. And this story has been widely circulated among the Jews to this very day.

The Great Commission

¹⁶Then the eleven disciples went to Galilee, to the mountain where Jesus had told them to go. ¹⁷When they saw him, they worshiped him; but some doubted. ¹⁸Then Jesus came to them and said, "All authority in heaven and on earth has been given to me. ¹⁹Therefore go and make disciples of all nations, baptizing them in the name of the Father and of the Son and of the Holy Spirit, ²⁰and teaching them to obey everything I have commanded you. And surely I am with you always, to the very end of the age."

4. What do you see as your role in carrying out the Great Commission?

5. How important is it to your faith that the tomb is empty? How would you explain the importance of the Resurrection to a non-Christian?

6. In your study on the life of Jesus, what is the key thing you learned about him and his ministry?

7. On a scale of 1 (baby steps) to 10 (giant leaps), how has your relationship with Christ progressed during the last three months?

CARING TIME

(Answer all the questions below, then take prayer requests and close with prayer.)

1. What was the "serendipity" (unexpected blessing) for you in this group?

2. What has the group decided to do next? What is the next step for you?

3. How would you like the group to continue praying for you?

Summary. The story of Jesus ends not with his death but with his resurrection. His death brought forgiveness for the sins of the world. His resurrection brought new life to humanity. Thus the story of Jesus is bounded on both ends by great miracles. It begins with the Incarnation (Jesus comes to planet earth). It ends with the Resurrection (and Ascension) as Jesus resumes his reign as the Lord of the universe. After Jesus died on the cross, his body was removed and placed in the tomb of Joseph, a member of the Sanhedrin who had opposed the action of the council (Matt. 27:57–61). The other council members, recalling how Jesus had predicted that he would rise from the dead, asked Pilate to post a guard around the tomb so that Jesus' disciples would not be able to steal the body and claim that Jesus had indeed risen from the dead (Matt. 27:62–66). Matthew then tells the story of what happened that third day. This passage tells the story of the Resurrection and the commissioning of the apostles to be Jesus' representatives throughout the world.

28:1 *After the Sabbath, at dawn on the first day of the week.* The Sabbath was considered over at 6 p.m. on Saturday. This scene takes place early on Sunday morning.

Mary Magdalene and the other Mary. While some of the Gospels mention other women who went to the tomb, all four Gospels place Mary Magdalene in a prominent role. See note on Mark 15:40 in Session 12. Mark mentions that the women brought aromatic oils to anoint the body, not so much to preserve it as to honor it (much like people today would put flowers on a grave). Clearly they did not expect Jesus to have risen from the dead, since they were shocked by what they found.

28:2 *a violent earthquake.* Earthquakes were often associated with manifestations of God's appearances on earth (Hab. 3:6).

an angel of the Lord … rolled back the stone. A tomb like this was cut out of the side of a hill. A large, disc-shaped stone was set in a groove so that it could be fairly easily rolled down to the opening to close it off. However, once in place it would have been very difficult for people to push it back up the incline.

28:3 Popular imagination often pictures angels as rather cute, chubby babies with wings or as weak, insipid, unhappy looking characters. However, throughout the Bible, angels are consistently described as majestic, awe-inspiring beings. Angels sometimes veiled their glory so that they were not recognized immediately as supernatural beings (e.g., Judg. 13:17–21). But whenever an angel appears in glory, the person or group who sees it reacts in the same way as these guards (v. 4).

lightning / white as snow. Brilliant, radiant light is often associated with appearances of God in the Old Testament. The angel reflects the glory of God.

28:4 The earthquake, the supernatural appearance of the angel, his feat of power, and his glory overwhelmed the guards. This was something entirely foreign to their experience and they were totally overcome by fear (see also Isa. 6:5; Dan. 10:7).

28:5 *Do not be afraid.* This, too, is the standard reply of an angel to the people to whom the angel is sent (Dan. 10:12; Luke 1:13,30; 2:10). While fear is an appropriate response to the glory of God, this is a word of grace to those the Lord calls to himself.

28:6 *he has risen.* In the same way that the Gospel writers report the crucifixion of Jesus in simple, stark terms (Matt. 27:35; Mark 15:24), so, too, they describe the Resurrection in a plain, unadorned way. The phrase literally reads "he has been raised," showing that God is the one who accomplished this great act. Jesus' resurrection demonstrates that the cry of the centurion was accurate: "Surely, this man was the Son of God!" (Matt. 27:54; Mark 15:39; see also Rom. 1:4).

Come and see the place where he lay. Typically, such tombs had a large antechamber, with a small two-foot-high doorway at the back which led into the six- or seven-foot burial chamber proper. This was the tomb of a wealthy family. See Isaiah 53:9, which says the Suffering Servant would be buried with the rich. The stone was rolled away not so that the resurrected Jesus could leave the tomb (he was already gone), but so that his disciples could see that it was empty (see John 20:8).

28:7 go / tell. Under Jewish law, women were not considered reliable witnesses. That they were the first to know of the resurrection was somewhat of an embarrassment to the early church (see Luke 24:11,22–24), hence guaranteeing this detail is historically accurate.

his disciples. They may have abandoned Jesus, but he has not abandoned them! Mark records that a special word was given to Peter. After his abysmal failure, Peter might have been tempted to count himself out of further discipleship.

into Galilee. Jesus said he would meet them again in Galilee (Matt. 26:32). The ministry of Jesus and the Twelve began in Galilee, and now they are directed back there to meet the risen Lord. This brings the account full circle.

28:8 afraid yet filled with joy. What they had experienced was radically unsettling. At the same time, the news delivered by the angel was so good they could scarcely believe it. Fear and joy were all mixed together.

28:9 worshiped him. This is the first mention in Matthew of people worshiping Jesus (see also v. 17). Whereas an angel rebukes John the apostle for bowing down to worship him (Rev. 22:8–9), Jesus accepts their worship. Since Jesus himself affirmed that only God should be worshiped (Matt. 4:10), this is a tacit acknowledgment of his divinity.

28:11–15 Only Matthew records this account of what the guards did after the Resurrection.

28:12 The Sanhedrin decided to try to buy off the Roman guards so that they would not tell what really happened.

28:13 You are to say. While verses 19–20 tell of Jesus' commission to his disciples, this is the Sanhedrin's commission to the guards. The disciples are motivated and encouraged in their task by the living presence of Jesus (v. 20), while the guards are motivated only by money.

His disciples came during the night and stole him away while we were asleep. This attempt at "damage control" was weak. The very reason the guards were posted was to keep the disciples from

trying to steal the body and concoct a story about resurrection. For a band of frightened men to be able to elude a Roman guard, roll the tombstone uphill without waking anyone, and steal away with the body stretched the limits of believability.

> *The presence of God with his people was always the goal toward which Israel looked under the old covenant. In Jesus, that presence is assured through the indwelling of Christ's Spirit.*

28:14 If this report gets to the governor. For a Roman guard to fall asleep on duty was an offense meriting execution. The Sanhedrin hopes Pilate will simply not find out about what happened. However, if the story they circulate reaches his ears, they will simply bribe him to forget about punishing the Roman soldiers.

28:15 this story has been widely circulated among the Jews to this very day. It is assumed that this Gospel was written around A.D. 80 about 50 years after this all took place. Today, the theory that Jesus' body was stolen by the disciples has been popularized by Hugh Schonfield's book, *The Passover Plot.*

28:16–20 Matthew returns to the main story as he sums up what happened when Jesus met with his disciples in Galilee.

28:16 to the mountain. We are not told which mountain this was. As was the case with the Transfiguration, the location of the mountain is not as significant as the theological meaning of mountains. See note on Mark 9:2 in Session 8.

28:17 some doubted. So stupendous, so without precedent, is the resurrection of Jesus that right from the beginning his disciples had difficulty accepting it. When the women reported what had happened at the tomb, the Eleven said it sounded like nonsense (Luke 24:9–11). After 10 of the disciples (all but Thomas) met the resurrected Jesus and

Notes (cont.)

believed (Luke 24:36–49), Thomas still doubted (John 20:24–29). Here, even while worshiping the resurrected Jesus, there is still some doubt.

28:18–20 This statement is known as the Great Commission. Because all authority in heaven and earth now belongs to Jesus, he sends his disciples to spread his message everywhere with the promise that he himself is with them to the end of time.

28:18 *All authority in heaven and on earth has been given to me.* This is the meaning of the statement "Jesus is Lord." Since there is no power greater than his (Rom. 8:38–39; Phil. 2:9–11; Col. 1:15–20), there is no other loyalty to which his disciples can give their absolute allegiance.

28:19 *go and make disciples.* Literally, this is "as you are going, make disciples." The point is not so much that the apostles are to travel far and wide, but that as they go about their business (whatever that is and wherever it takes them), they are to be teaching people about Jesus and his kingdom. This is to be their pressing concern.

of all nations. The inclusive nature of Jesus' mission is crystal-clear: his kingdom includes all types of people. There are no geographic, racial, ethnic or national realms that are outside of the authority and concern of Jesus.

in the name of the Father and of the Son and of the Holy Spirit. This is a clear trinitarian formula. While the doctrine of the Trinity was not clearly articulated and defined until the third century, the roots of its teaching are clearly seen here. There is one name (or character) that defines the triune God. To be baptized "in his name" (literally "into the name") means to enter into fellowship with him.

28:20 *I am with you always.* This is the climactic promise of the new covenant. The presence of God with his people was always the goal toward which Israel looked under the old covenant. In Jesus, that presence is assured through the indwelling of Christ's Spirit (John 14:16–17).

to the very end of the age. This covers all time until the return of Christ when the new heaven and new earth will be revealed.

Acknowledgments

It is not possible (nor desirable) to tackle as formidable a subject as the Life of Christ without the aid of others. The standard exegetical tools have, of course, been used: *The Arndt and Gingrich Greek-English Lexicon of the New Testament*; *The Interpreter's Dictionary of the Bible*, etc. In addition, reference has been made to a series of fine commentaries: Albright and Mann, *The Gospel of Matthew* (The Anchor Bible Series), Garden City, NY: Doubleday and Co., 1971. Brown, Colin, *"Miracle,"* *Dictionary of New Testament Theology*, Vol. 11, Grand Rapids, MI: Zondervan, 1978. Brown, Raymond, *The Gospel of John* (The Anchor Bible Series), Garden City, NY: Doubleday and Co., 1970. Cranfield, C.E.B., *St. Mark*, London: Cambridge, 1939. Douglas, J.D., *The New Bible Dictionary*, Grand Rapids, MI: Eerdmans, 1973. Lane, William, *Commentary on the Gospel of Mark* (The New International Commentary on the New Testament), Grand Rapids, MI: Eerdmans, 1974. Mann, C.S., *Mark* (The Anchor Bible Series), Garden City, NY: Doubleday and Co., 1986. Marshall, I. Howard, *Commentary on Luke* (The New International Greek Testament Commentary), Grand Rapids, MI: William B. Eerdmans, 1978. Hill, David, *The Gospel of Matthew* (The New Century Bible Commentary), Grand Rapids, MI: William B. Eerdmans, 1972. France, R.T., *Matthew* (Tyndale New Testament Commentaries), Grand Rapids, MI: William B. Eerdmans, 1985. Mounce, Robert H., *Matthew* (A Good News Commentary), San Francisco: Harper & Row, 1985. Guelich, Robert A., Mark 1:8–26 (Word Biblical Commentary), Dallas, TX: Word Publishers, 1989. Hendriksen, William, *The Gospel of Luke* (New Testament Commentary), Grand Rapids, MI: Baker Book House, 1978. Hendriksen, William, *The Gospel of John* (New Testament Commentary), Grand Rapids, MI: Baker Book House, 1953. Morris, Leon, *The Gospel According to John* (The New International Commentary on the New Testament), Grand Rapids, MI: William B. Eerdmans, 1971. Michaels, J. Ramsey, *John* (A Good News Commentary), San Francisco: Harper & Row, 1984.

Caring Time Notes